What America Needs

WHAT AMERICA NEEDS

THE CASE FOR TRUMP

JEFFREY LORD

REGNERY
PUBLISHING
A Division of Salem Media Group

Regnery® is a registered trademark of Salem Communications Holding Corporation

Cataloging-in-Publication data on file with the Library of Congress

ISBN 978-1-62157-523-8

Published in the United States by
Regnery Publishing
A Division of Salem Media Group
300 New Jersey Ave NW
Washington, DC 20001
www.Regnery.com

Manufactured in the United States of America

10 9 8 7 6 5 4 3 2 1

Books are available in quantity for promotional or premium use. For information on discounts and terms, please visit our website: www.Regnery.com.

Distributed to the trade by
Perseus Distribution
250 West 57th Street
New York, NY 10107

Donald Trump's position papers reprinted with permission. For more information, go to https://www.donaldjtrump.com/positions.

For my mother, Kathleen J. Lord—
at ninety-six still encouraging her son.
And my dad, Nelville B. "Buzz" Lord—
no longer here but always present.

CONTENTS

Introduction

Appearing on Fox News Channel's *Special Report with Bret Baier*, *Washington Post* columnist George Will was asked how much he would bet in the show's "Candidate Casino" on various potential 2016 Republican candidates. Replied Will: "One dollar on Donald Trump in the hope that he will be tempted to run, be predictably shellacked, and we will be spared evermore this quadrennial charade of his."

Will has called Trump an "unprecedentedly and incorrigibly vulgar presidential candidate." And he's not alone. Kevin Williamson of *National Review* has called Trump a "witless ape" who grunts "like a baboon." Williamson (who is apparently unaware that Abraham Lincoln was frequently scorned as a "gorilla" by his critics and contemptuously derided as a "well meaning baboon" by no less than Union General George McClellan) also wrote about imagining a Trump sex tape. Such is his chivalry, he referred to the beautiful Melania Trump as Donald Trump's "plastic-surgery-disaster wife." His colleague at *National Review*, Rich Lowry, was equally high-minded, saying in late September 2015 that in a recent debate Carly Fiorina had cut Trump's "balls off." If, two months later, as Lowry sat down to his Thanksgiving Dinner, he happened to look at the polls, he would see Trump still leading the field, with Carly Fiorina mired in the single digits—so much for pundit prescience.

Many on the Right were so exasperated by Trump's success that they actually asked if he was a Democrat plant; others, less conspiracy-minded, simply dismissed Trump as an embarrassment. Barely a month into Trump's candidacy, the *Wall Street Journal*'s editorial page cheerfully predicted his "inevitable self-immolation." The paper's owner, media mogul Rupert Murdoch, tweeted:

"When is Donald Trump going to stop embarrassing his friends, let alone the whole country?" The mainstream media, and almost every pundit left and right—with a few singular exceptions, like Charles Hurt at the *Washington Times*—have shown how out of touch they are with the American people by their humiliatingly wrong, yet endlessly repeated, predictions that Trump's popularity was a blip that would be gone in an instant. The reality is that Donald Trump has soared to the top of the polls—and stayed there because he has a message that resonates with the American people. The media might mock Trump for saying, "We will have so much winning if I get elected you may get bored with winning," but to the American people it seems like we haven't "won" for a long time, let alone had a president who put our nation's security and prosperity first, and Trump, at least, is willing to try.

His so-called "vulgarity" is seen by most Americans as honesty—the same sort of honesty that the American people saw in such alleged vulgarians as Andrew Jackson, Abraham Lincoln, and Harry Truman whom the American people regarded as tough, plain-speaking leaders; and Trump has certainly been no more "vulgar" than his critics.

The fact is, Trump's connection with the American people is real. His appearances have attracted record-breaking crowds, filling vast athletic arenas with tens of thousands of enthusiastic supporters, and his appeal has boosted the stature of other anti-Establishment Republicans. In the 2015 Kentucky governor's race, for instance, Republican Matt Bevin, written off by the pundits as a sure loser, won in a landslide, and a chastened Democrat operative ascribed the victory to "Trump-mania."

As 2015 came to a close, the *Washington Post* reported that "there is growing anxiety bordering on panic among Republican elites about the dominance and durability of Donald Trump...."

Why is the Republican Establishment afraid of the party's most popular candidate? Don't they want to win? And why is a blunt-talking businessman, who has never held public office, the most likely Republican, as I write, to win the party's nomination and perhaps the presidency itself?

The answer is that there is a vast chasm between the average American voter and the political class—and Trump, more effectively than anyone else, has leapt to the voters' side. As Charles Hurt noted in the *Washington Times*: "Donald Trump—the great salesman-statesman—

not only intimately understands the product he is selling (himself), he also has a deeply instinctual understanding of his customer (voters). He understands what they want, how they think and how to reach them."

The Republican Establishment looks to manipulate the average American to get his vote and get reelected; making good on policy promises is much less important than simply holding office and playing up to the media. Trump the billionaire, ironically and by contrast, shares the concerns of the average American and gives him a voice—saying what, to the Establishment, is unsayable about immigration, trade, and terrorism, among other topics; and voters believe he means it and will act on it.

Political pundits live in a world of ideas and, all too frequently, cynical speculation about hidden motives. We like slick policy statements and detailed policy-wonk interviews, because it makes our job seem important— not that it isn't! But the average American voter is much more concerned about a leader's priorities and his commitment to action. Trump has the average American's priorities—he wants to make America great again, after more than a decade of apparent decline. And unlike the politicians in Washington, he seems a man of resolute action, and not someone who will be intimidated by opposition or the media.

Millions of those Trump-supporting average Americans have had enough. They are tired of being dismissed as rubes, nativists, xenophobes, gun nuts, and anti-immigrant racists by the media and the political class. They agree with Trump that the Establishment has proven itself to be "incompetent" at best or simply "stupid." It's hard to imagine how Donald Trump could do worse—and there are many reasons, which I've narrowed down to seven, to think that he could do much, much better and be the president America needs to meet this nation's most pressing challenges.

America Needs a Defender

When Mexico sends its people, they're not sending their best.... They're sending people that have lots of problems, and they're bringing those problems.... They're bringing drugs. They're bringing crime. They're rapists. And some, I assume, are good people.

—Donald Trump, announcing his presidential campaign, June 16, 2015

Donald Trump's remarks about illegal immigrants from Mexico, remarks made in his speech announcing his candidacy, launched the proverbial political firestorm. The political, business, and media Establishment threw a fit—accusing Trump, the husband, son, and grandson of immigrants, of being "anti-immigrant" when in fact he is opposed to *illegal* immigration.

Tellingly, not only is the Establishment so corrupt that it has no interest in abiding by the law, or making the distinction between legal and illegal immigration, but the very first reaction from Trump's critics was to strike out at Trump financially; in other words, not to debate the issue, but to intimidate him into silence. Univision abruptly canceled its contract with Trump to carry the Trump-owned Miss Universe and Miss USA pageants. Likewise NBC, the network that had televised his famous *Apprentice* shows, severed its longtime ties to Trump. The network issued a statement that said: "Due to the recent derogatory statements by Donald Trump regarding immigrants, NBCUniversal is ending its business relationship with Mr. Trump. At NBC, respect and dignity for all people are cornerstones of our values." Note well that NBC changed Trump's point about *illegal* immigrants and remade it into the straw man of "immigrants."

So too did Macy's play the straw man game, announcing the department store chain would no longer be carrying Trump's signature ties and menswear collection, sniffing: "We welcome all customers, and respect for the dignity of all people is a cornerstone of our culture. We are disappointed and distressed by recent remarks about immigrants from Mexico.... In light of statements made by Donald Trump...we have decided to discontinue our business relationship."

Almost immediately Trump's poll numbers began to soar.

Why?

Because Americans understood Trump's plainspoken words were accurate. America, a nation based not on racial or ethnic identity but on principles of freedom and liberty, is the only country in the world whose population is filled 100 percent with the descendants of immigrants. The problem is not immigration, per se, but *illegal* immigration. The president of the National Border Patrol Council says that 20 percent of illegals captured at the border have a criminal record.

We've actually known for a long time that illegal immigrants are disproportionately likely to commit crimes in the United States, but the political Establishment has done little or nothing about it.

Heather Mac Donald of the Manhattan Institute reported as long ago as 2004 that, for example, in "Los Angeles, 95 percent of all outstanding warrants for homicide (which total 1,200 to 1,500) target illegal aliens. Up to two-thirds of all fugitive felony warrants (17,000) are for illegal aliens." Trump knows that, the American people know that, but the political Establishment wants to sweep such statistics under the rug, regardless of what that means for American citizens.

But it is no longer possible to limit this debate to illegal immigration. Ann Coulter's recent book ¡*Adios, America!: The Left's Plan to Turn Our Country into a Third World Hellhole* is a veritable encyclopedia of statistics on problems surrounding both illegal and legal immigration.

As Trump noted in his detailed immigration plan: "In 2011, the Government Accountability Office found that there were a shocking 3 million arrests attached to the incarcerated alien population, including tens of thousands of violent beatings, rapes and murders."

One man in particular knew exactly how accurate Trump's words were.

At 8:40 p.m. on Sunday, March 2, 2008, seventeen-year-old Jamiel Shaw Jr. was walking home from the mall with two friends. Jamiel's combination of athletic prowess—he was a Los Angeles high school football star—and high academics were already drawing attention from Stanford and Rutgers.

He was three doors away from home when a white car pulled up. Inside were 18th Street Gang members Joel "Killer" Rodriguez, Ysenia Sanchez, and Pedro "Darky" Espinoza. Espinoza jumped out and approached Jamiel.

Born in Mexico and brought to America when he was three years old by his illegal immigrant (and allegedly abusive) parents, Pedro "Darky" Espinoza had joined the 18th Street Gang specifically to become a killer; he told his parole officer his ambition was to land on death row.

Darky had been released from prison only the day before, after serving time for assault with a deadly weapon. Now, he had already obtained another gun—in a state with the toughest gun control laws in the country.

Jamiel had been on his cell phone, talking with his girlfriend Chrystale Miles. He suddenly stopped talking. Chrystale could hear a voice demand of Jamiel, "Where you from?" Before Jamiel could respond, Darky pulled the gun and shot Jamiel in the stomach. As the seventeen-year-old lay on the sidewalk writhing in pain, Darky Espinoza stood over him, pointed the gun at Jamiel's head execution-style and pulled the trigger.

Jamiel's father, Jamiel Shaw Sr., heard the gunshots and ran out of his house, fearing the worst. The local NBC affiliate later reported, "The first law enforcement officer on the scene, a veteran LAPD sergeant, said the scene of Shaw's murder was 'the most sorrow and despair I've ever seen,' describing the sight of Jamiel Shaw Sr. screaming in agony at the sight of his son's body."

Jamiel's mother, Army Sergeant Anita Shaw, called home from Iraq in desperate hope that there was some mistake, that her "baby" had not been cold-bloodedly murdered. She sobbed, "Tell me it's not my son."

Six days later Pedro "Darky" Espinoza was arrested and charged with the murder of Jamiel Andre Shaw Jr.

When Trump took the podium to announce his candidacy, and denounced illegal aliens who were "bringing crime" to American streets, he did so with the desire to protect families like the Shaws.

Famously, Trump also pledged to build a wall along America's southern border: "I would build a great wall, and nobody builds walls better than me, believe me, and I'll build them very inexpensively, I will build a great, great wall on our southern border. And I will have Mexico pay for that wall. Mark my words."

But Trump has more in mind than building a wall. He intends to immediately deport the illegal aliens who prey on our citizens and are incarcerated in our prisons. An emphatic Trump told Bill O'Reilly: "If I'm elected, they're going to be out of here day one. We're going to get them the hell out of our country. They're going to be out so fast your head will spin."

Trump went even further. He proposed to deport every illegal immigrant in the country, not just the illegal immigrant felons sitting in our jails, specifically citing the success of President Dwight D. Eisenhower's program in the 1950s, "Operation Wetback," which rounded up and deported illegal aliens. In 2006, the *Christian Science*

Monitor took a retrospective look at the Eisenhower program and noted:

> Fifty-three years ago, when newly elected Dwight Eisenhower moved into the White House, America's southern frontier was as porous as a spaghetti sieve. As many as 3 million illegal migrants had walked and waded northward over a period of several years for jobs in California, Arizona, Texas, and points beyond.
>
> President Eisenhower cut off this illegal traffic. He did it quickly and decisively with only 1,075 United States Border Patrol agents— less than one-tenth of today's force. The operation is still highly praised among veterans of the Border Patrol.

Today, of course, we're told that such effective enforcement of our immigration laws and our borders is impossible, and certainly the massive Washington bureaucracy and its lawyer-class would try to make it so. But Trump, to his credit, doesn't listen to naysayers. He is used to getting things done, and he knows that what America did once, it can do again.

So the focus of the media and the political Establishment now is to discredit Operation Wetback. The *New York Times* all too predictably launched a hysterical attack on Trump for his position on deporting illegals. Said the paper, "Because his plan is so naked—in its scapegoating of immigrants, its barely subtextual racism, its immense cruelty in seeking to reduce millions of people to poverty and hopelessness—it gives his opponents the chance for a very clear moral decision. They can stand up for better values, and against the collective punishment of millions of innocent Americans-in-waiting." What did the *Times* conveniently leave out? In the day—meaning the Truman and Eisenhower era—the *Times* was an enthusiastic supporter of deporting illegals. To cite but one example from March 28, 1951, when Democrat Harry Truman was trying to deport illegals—the paper accused American growers who supported illegal immigration of supporting "peonage"—which is to say, the paper saw illegal immigration as a first cousin to slavery. A year later the *Times* was calling the presence of illegals in America a—wait for it—"wetback invasion." It would go on to lavish favorable publicity on the Eisenhower mass deportation program.

Not only did Eisenhower's "Operation Wetback" have a politically incorrect name, but, now its critics allege, it was cruel in rounding up Mexican nationals and returning them to their own country. The *Washington Post* reported, for instance, that "After one such round-up and transfer in July, 88 people died from heat stroke."

Certainly, the deaths of eighty-eight people represent a tragedy (though a tragedy that lies much more at the doorstep of Mexico). Yet to use that as evidence to oppose Trump's immigration plan is to ignore the deaths that result from our current immigration disaster—not just among American citizens, about whom the Establishment appears to care so little, but among the illegal immigrants themselves. Here is the *New York Times* in 2013 on the brutal reality of illegal immigration today:

TUCSON—In the Pima County Medical Examiner's Office here—repository of the nation's largest collection of missing-person reports for immigrants who have vanished while crossing the United States-Mexico border—774 sets of remains awaited identification in mid-May, stored in musty body bags coated in dust.

. . . the largest number of the deaths last year occurred along the punishing stretch of desert that spans the southernmost tip of the Border Patrol's Tucson sector, the busiest along the border.

. . . Assembling the remains, like linking a mandible that arrived in the office early this spring to a set of remains that was missing one, is like solving a grisly puzzle. It requires manually searching the color-coded paper case files lining the walls in Dr. Anderson's office: one shelf for cases from the late 1990s, when there were few, and the rest for the more than 2,100 deaths since 2001.

Illegal immigration's victims lie on both sides of the border. It is simply wrong to put American lives at risk; and it is equally wrong to leave our border so undefended that illegal aliens are tempted to risk their lives, and often lose their lives, trying to make the journey (often through the agency of unscrupulous and abusive people-smugglers).

Until Donald Trump raised the subject, confronting the human costs of illegal immigration was a third rail that few politicians dared touch; and certainly no one has addressed the issue as frankly as Trump has done.

Among the millions of Americans who appreciate his honesty about illegal immigration and his compassion for illegal immigration's victims, are the parents of Jamiel Shaw. They met with Donald Trump and publicly endorsed him, because they felt that until Trump came along, no one was willing to tell the truth about the crimes of illegal immigrants. Jamiel Shaw Sr. sat down with Fox News' Neil Cavuto and told him that "for the first time" since his son was murdered, he and fellow victims of illegal immigrant felons "feel hope, we feel change coming."

He added, "Donald Trump brought in fresh air, Donald Trump…made us think like, 'Oh, you know, maybe we have a chance to get our country back, or at least make the citizens safe.' That if you're going to force this illegal immigration down our throat, at least you owe us the safety part of it to make sure our loved ones aren't being murdered in the streets."

The political Establishment had not previously shown much concern for families like the Shaws. When Anita Shaw said that "I felt everyone was trying to keep it quiet, I felt like because he [Pedro Espinoza] was an illegal alien it was alright that he killed my son," she was not wrong.

From the U.S. Chamber of Commerce to the *Wall Street Journal* to Establishment Republicans, let alone the liberal Democrats who see electoral gains to be made through massive demographic change, the push has been on for what is called "comprehensive immigration reform," seen by millions of Americans as nothing short of amnesty for all illegal aliens, and even a move to put them at the front of the line, ahead of those who have followed the law and played by the rules.

To the Establishment, borders are almost a scandal.

The response of Donald Trump: "If we don't have borders we don't have a country."

★   ★   ★

As Trump's campaign gained steam in the summer of 2015, thirty-two-year-old Kate Steinle took a stroll in scenic San Francisco with her father—only to be abruptly shot to death in broad daylight. The shooter was quickly captured, and was revealed to be a five-time deportee named Francisco Sanchez.

Had Trump not raised the issue of illegal immigration to the forefront, this story too might have been swept under the rug by the politically correct media. But instead, the murder became a source of national outrage. How could American cities, like San Francisco, think so little of their own American citizens as to provide "sanctuary" for illegal immigrants like Francisco Sanchez?

The issues of illegal immigration and "Sanctuary Cities" like San Francisco where immigration law was not enforced surged to the top of the polls. One typical poll, this one from CNN, had 44 percent of Republicans believing Trump was the best candidate to handle the immigration issue. No one else came close.

★ ★ ★

This could be the greatest Trojan horse. This could make the Trojan horse look like peanuts if these people turned out to be a lot of ISIS.

—Donald Trump explaining his opposition to President Obama's plan to allow thousands of Syrian refugees into America

Into the already explosive issue of illegal immigration came the issue of Syrian refugees. With ISIS running rampant through the Middle East, there was a sudden surge of refugees as hundreds of thousands tried to flee to Europe. President Obama announced that he intended to bring as many as ten thousand Syrian refugees to America.

In October 2015 Trump responded directly to the issue, criticizing the injection of thousands of Syrian refugees into Germany, and Germany's commitment to take no fewer than eight hundred thousand immigrants. He called that policy of accepting mass migration "insane." His alternative was to establish "safe zones" in the Middle East to house the refugees—a policy that would protect Europe from a massive flood of immigrants and allow the refugees to resettle closer to their original homes, and in Muslim lands that seem, right now, to be doing very little to help their neighbors.

Trump believes, as do most serious analysts, that many of the alleged refugees from the Muslim world pose security threats to Europe and the United States. Putting America first, he said he would flatly refuse to take Syrian refugees into America if he were president. Far from being all widows and orphans, as President Barack

Obama described them, Trump correctly noted that the "refugees" seemed mostly to be young men. He said, "I've been watching this migration. And I see the people. I mean, they're men, they're mostly men, and…what I won't do is take in 200,000 Syrians who could be ISIS."

One month later, on November 13, 2015, ISIS terrorists struck in Paris, killing 130 and wounding 350. One of the dead was twenty-three-year-old Nohemi Gonzalez, a young American student studying design in a year abroad from California State University, Long Beach. Among the Paris killers, exactly as Trump had warned, was twenty-five-year-old Ahmed Almuhamed, a Syrian who had entered Europe nestled in a throng of Syrian "refugees" that had made their way to France from the island of Leros in Greece, a mere seven miles from Turkey.

The refugees arrived in boats, and Almuhamed's boat had capsized before he was rescued by the Europeans he later tried to kill. In due course it was confirmed that a second ISIS terrorist involved in the Paris attack had arrived with Syrian refugees. Another four of the terrorists had spent time in Syria.

In the aftermath of the Paris attack, Trump's earlier warning of a "Trojan horse" seemed prophetic, even if it was only common sense—common sense lacking in the media and political Establishment. Said Trump to CNBC, "We cannot let them into this country, period. Our country has tremendous problems. We can't have another problem."

Unfortunately, a mere nineteen days later, Trump was proved, tragically, right again.

On December 2, 2015, fourteen Americans were mass murdered in San Bernardino, California, while attending an office Christmas party. The location was the Inland Regional Center, a California state government center for those working with the disabled. Another twenty-one of the office workers were injured. An image tweeted out from the party before the attack showed one office worker, a woman, sitting on the knee of a Santa Claus—next to a Christmas tree: symbols of the Christian holiday celebrating the birth of Christ.

The two shooters, who conducted a military-style assault on the gathering and were later shot dead by the police, were shortly revealed to have been husband and wife Islamic radicals—the very embodiment of the term President Obama refuses even to say aloud. The wife—the personification of Trump's warning about a "Trojan horse" Islamic radical allowed into the country—was twenty-seven-year-old Tashfeen Malik. A Pakistani woman raised in Saudi Arabia, Malik entered America on a "K-1" visa, dubbed the "fiancé visa" because current immigration law allows a foreigner into the country for ninety days if the intent is to marry an American citizen— a marriage which in turn changes the legal status of the immigrant to allow him or her to apply for "permanent resident" status. Malik had done just this, marrying her native-born American Muslim husband Syed Farook, the son of Pakistani immigrants. Together the two plotted the attack on the Inland Regional Center—where Syed Farook himself was an employee. When authorities swarmed their home, they discovered what one official grimly called an "IED factory" littered with pipe bombs and explosives.

Trump sees the problems with the clarity of 20-20 vision and common sense, a common sense shared by millions of Americans. But too many in our political Establishment continue to willfully ignore them. President Obama, for one, continues to be determined to import thousands of Syrian refugees into America. In the aftermath of yet another Islamic radical attack on America, Obama and other liberals focused not on the entrance of Islamic radicals into America, but, unbelievably, on gun control, as if Islamic radicals intent on jihad are going to obey any gun law. Even after the Chairman of the House Subcommittee on Terrorism had to confess to *Fox News Sunday* host Chris Wallace that "There's virtually no vetting" of the Syrian refugees Obama wants to import to the United States. "There are no databases in Syria. There are no government records."

The oath of office of the president of the United States reads as follows: "I do solemnly swear that I will faithfully execute the Office of President of the United States, and will to the best of my ability, preserve, protect and defend the Constitution of the United States."

To "defend the Constitution of the United States" begins with defending the borders of the United States. The first reason why America needs Donald Trump is that he would put an end to illegal immigration—and take a hard look at our legal immigration system. He would build an effective wall along our southern border, and he would not take risks with our immigration policies that would allow ISIS fighters or sympathizers like Tashfeen Malik to enter our country. He would work diligently to remove any who might already be here, in part by stricter enforcement of our visa laws, by strengthening those laws, and by tripling the number of Immigration and Customs Enforcement officers. Donald Trump would not wink at, or tolerate, such lawlessness as sanctuary cities. Instead, he would strip them of federal funds until they followed our immigration laws. He would not perpetuate a federal policy of "catch and release" for illegal aliens but would instead, again, enforce our immigration laws and deport every person who is here illegally, including a "mandatory return of all criminal aliens" to their home countries—in stark contrast to the Obama administration policy of simply releasing tens of thousands of aliens with criminal convictions. More than that, Trump would reform our current immigration laws so that the interests of America's citizens come before the interests of would-be immigrants. Among his reforms: ending "birthright" citizenship (which attracts illegal immigrants here in the first place), terminating welfare for non-citizens, and requiring American companies to hire American workers first.

But more than his detailed policy proposals, for which he has, typically, been given little credit by the mainstream media, Trump has shown something else: courage and commitment that we don't often see in politicians. Despite the inevitable catcalls of racism, despite the attempt by Univision, NBC, and Macy's to punish

Trump by severing their business relationships with him, despite endless criticism from the mainstream media, Trump has never wavered. That is why he might be the one chief executive who can get the job done.

Donald Trump will first and foremost be America's Defender.

REASON TWO

America Needs a Truth-Teller

My father's not politically correct, he says what he means and he means what he says, and I think that's the way the American people are.

—Ivanka Trump

★　　★　　★

"**C**ross a liberal on duty, and he becomes a man of hurtling irrationality." So wrote the late William F.
Buckley Jr. in a slender volume of political thought
circa 1959 titled *Up from Liberalism*. Suffice to say, the
"hurtling irrationality" that Buckley observed a full fifty-
seven years ago (when Donald Trump was thirteen years
old) has not merely gained steam. In the guise of "political
correctness" and combined with "identity politics" it has
become a vast intolerance engulfing the nation, heavily
layered with the Left's traditional and virulent out and
out racism that requires everyone to be judged by skin
color.

And if you think that's painting with too broad a
brush, try to think about—honestly—the last time you
met a liberal who truly judged someone by the content of
his or her character rather than the color of their skin.
The Left makes—and has always made—its political living exacerbating racial tensions, highlighting racial differences, promoting race-favoring policies, and taking
race into account, albeit for different ends, as much as the
South African apartheid regime ever did.

In the current leftist jargon, they do all this to compensate for "White Privilege." In fact, they use it not just to promote programs like race-based affirmative action and not just to inculcate a sense of victimhood in every group in America save for straight, white, Christian males, but to shut down debate, disallow dissenting voices, and ignore or rewrite history. In fact, the very idea of "White Privilege" is about "Liberal Privilege"—the right of the American Left to define problems in terms of leftist dogma, forcing the rest of America to dance according to the Left's rules of dance.

But did you know that *the* poorest county in America is overwhelmingly *white*, or that many *white* American settlers came here as indentured servants or as impoverished immigrants or scratched a living from the land as tenant farmers (working side by side with blacks), or that fewer than 5 percent of all whites in the antebellum South owned slaves (and so by the way did a few blacks and so did Indians)?

No, I didn't think so. But you could have learned these truths from, among other sources, former Reagan Secretary of the Navy and former conservative Democrat candidate for president Jim Webb, a former U.S. senator from Virginia, who has written eloquently on the subject of the "myth of white privilege"—and you saw how the

Democrats treated him; they decided he had no place in their party.

Like Jim Webb, but on a far bigger playing field, Donald Trump will not play the Left's game of racial pandering or of perpetuating falsehoods about the reality of American history—an important battlefield because what we think of the past determines what policies we, as people, favor in the future. The Left has a tremendous investment and interest in making American history seem like a litany of sexism and racism that only they can cure. They are about the eternal rule of Liberal Privilege. America needs a truth-teller who won't let that happen.

From his speeches to his tweets, Donald Trump has shown he is fearless in defying the Left's attempt to shut down debate. He is more than willing to state, baldly, and in language a truck driver can agree with, an obvious truth whether it is politically incorrect or not.

For example, on President Obama and the Baltimore riots, Trump tweeted:

> Our great African American President hasn't exactly had a positive impact on the thugs who are so happily and openly destroying Baltimore!
> —@realDonaldTrump, April 27, 2015

On Jeb Bush:

…So true. Jeb Bush is crazy, who cares that he speaks Mexican, this is America, English!!
—@realDonaldTrump, August 24, 2015

On global warming:

This very expensive GLOBAL WARMING bullshit has got to stop. Our planet is freezing, record low temps, and our GW scientists are stuck in ice.
—@realDonaldTrump, January 1, 2014

Trump is often attacked for not being a policy wonk, yet the press, and sometimes his Republican opponents, have repeatedly tried to nail him on non-policy questions—starting with the giant dust-up after Fox anchor and debate questioner Megyn Kelly asked him about sexist comments he had allegedly made. Trump called the question unfair and asserted that Kelly was out to get him. He told CNN's Don Lemon, "You could see there was blood coming out of her eyes. Blood coming out of her wherever…." When critics accused him of implying that Kelly's harsh questioning of him was driven by her menstrual cycle, he responded appropriately, "Only a deviant would say that what I said was what they were referring to, because nobody would make that statement. You almost have to be sick to put that together." Or as he told another interviewer, "Only a sick person would even think about it."

For the record he said he meant to say "nose"—and never came close to saying what his critics suggested, which perhaps says more about them than him. Maybe more important than Trump's spat with Kelly over her questioning of him was his use of the word "deviant," a word unlikely to pass any other politician's lips these days, but another sign that he's willing to tell it like it is—especially to the gutter-minded press.

Or remember his assessment that Jeb Bush was "low energy" (which seems true enough) or that Rand Paul "reminds me of a spoiled brat without a properly functioning brain," in other words, an ideologue raised by an ideologue.

If the American public has learned anything about Trump in the course of his presidential campaign it is, as his daughter Ivanka has noted, that he has no time for political correctness. To which his supporters respond

with hosannas, because there is nothing rarer in a politician—and it is not just politicians who are affected.

Political correctness dominates not just our politics,
but the media, business, religion, governmental regula-
tion, and to an almost unimaginable degree the schools
and colleges and universities to which we send our young
people. In the "home of the free" we are every day *less*
free to say what we actually think—or even to tell the
truth, if the truth deviates from the leftist party line. We
are talking about a form of tyranny that few Republicans
are willing to fight. Instead, they all too often go along
when the Left abridges the First Amendment rights of free
speech and freedom of religion (or, to pick up an issue of
2015, de facto bans of the Confederate battle flag, though
the flag of ISIS is okay) in the name of banning "hate
speech." (And not to be too obvious, the Confederate flag
was for generations in essence the political banner of
the Democrats—the Democrats who opposed even the
Thirteenth Amendment that abolished slavery, not to
mention every Republican-sponsored pro–civil rights
constitutional amendment or statute that did everything
from giving ex-slaves the right to vote to eat in public
restaurants.) Much of Donald Trump's popularity can be

linked to the very fact that he is willing to fight this tyranny by saying exactly what he thinks, without apology.

It is a serious problem—recognized even by fair-minded liberals, like Kirsten Powers, who wrote about the issue at length in her book, the 2015 bestseller *The Silencing*, where she recounts, as an insider and a political commentator, just how willing the Left is to smear opponents and try to shut down a free exchange and debate of ideas.

In the name of political correctness demands have been made to fire Rush Limbaugh, delegitimize Fox News, and fire this or that university president or professor who disagrees with the Left's agenda. The tentacles of this particularly vicious strain of soft totalitarianism have spread wide.

Indeed, so iron-fisted is the political correctness regime that already in a still young 2016 campaign Hillary Clinton has felt the need to abjectly apologize for using the phrase "illegal immigrants." While another Democrat, former Maryland Governor Martin O'Malley, profusely apologized for daring to say "all lives matter." Clearly, in the world of political correctness, they don't, as the Black Lives Matter movement was quick to point out to him.

It is tempting to write political correctness off as largely a campus phenomenon or something to joke about or no more harmful than maybe telling white lies or using certain jargon to avoid giving offense.

But it is much more serious than that. It is an attempt to control not just what we say, but what we think. And in its extremism it guides the policies of our government in ways that can actually endanger American lives.

It is political correctness enforced by the Obama administration that forbids us, for example, from acknowledging radical Islam as a source of terrorism. That is a governmental omission that has already cost American lives. On December 2, 2015, this cost fourteen lives in San Bernardino, California, when a neighbor confessed she was suspicious of the activities of Tashfeen Malik and Syed Farook but was reluctant to report them because of a politically correct fear of being accused of racism. Trump has long warned of this kind of danger, saying of this politically correct reluctance to report the two, "Can anybody be that dumb? We've become so politically correct that we don't know what the hell we're doing."

On November 5, 2009, U.S. Army Major Nidal Hasan walked onto his base at Fort Hood, Texas, armed with an FN Five-seven pistol outfitted with two laser sights. Taking a seat at an empty table in the Soldier Readiness Processing Center, Hasan bowed his head for a moment as if in prayer. Then he stood up, shouted "Allahu Akbar!," and began spraying the room with gunfire. Systematically aiming for soldiers in uniform, Hasan killed twelve soldiers and one civilian, with thirty people being wounded. Hasan himself was finally shot, bringing his rampage to an end and paralyzing him for life.

Investigations would eventually show that both the army and the FBI were well aware that Hasan had terrorist sympathies. In the aftermath of the Fort Hood shooting, Fox News reported on how political correctness had prevented the authorities from intervening against Hasan before his rampage:

> "There were definitely clear indications that Hasan's loyalties were not with America," Lt. Col. Val Finnell, Hasan's classmate at the Uniformed Services University of the Health Sciences in Bethesda, Md., told FoxNews.com in an exclusive interview. He and Hasan were students in the school's public health master's degree program from 2007–2008.

"There were all sorts of…comments made throughout the year that made me question his loyalty to the United States, but nothing was done," said Finnell, who recalled one class during which Hasan gave a presentation justifying homicide bombings.

"The issue here is that there's a political correctness climate in the military. They don't want to say anything because it would be considered questioning somebody's religious belief, or they're afraid of an equal opportunity lawsuit.

"I want to be clear that this wasn't about anyone questioning his religious views. It is different when you are a civilian than when you are a military officer," said Finnell, who is a physician at the Los Angeles Air Force Base.

"When you are in the military and you start making comments that are seditious, when you say you believe something other than your oath of office—someone needed to say why is this guy saying this stuff.

"He was a lightning rod. He made his views known and he was very vocal, he had extremely radical jihadist views," Finnell said. "When you're a military officer you take an oath to defend against all enemies foreign and domestic.

"They should've confronted him—our professors, officers—but they were too concerned about being politically correct."

In other words, thirteen Americans, twelve of them American soldiers, were shot to death on an American military base in the middle of Texas because the U.S. Army was infected with the virus of political correctness. Incredibly, the army classified Hasan's murderous spree as "workplace violence," and the first reaction of General Martin Dempsey, then the army chief of staff, was to say, "as horrific as this tragedy was, if our diversity becomes a casualty, I think that's worse." The entire Obama administration recited from these outrageous "diversity is our strength" talking points. Political correctness is more important, to the Left, than are American lives. Not only does Trump not share this position, he has spoken out forcefully against how political correctness is impeding our fight against radical Islam. He has said that "political correctness is killing us in this country," and told Bill O'Reilly in 2012 in response to a question about whether there is "a Muslim problem in the world": "Absolutely, absolutely…and that's the sad part…because you have fabulous Muslims—I know many Muslims, and they are fabulous people, they're smart, they're industrious. Unfortunately…there is a Muslim problem in the world."

Time moves on, but political correctness has only intensified its grip on American political debate. At an August 2015 press conference in Dubuque, Iowa, Trump stood at a podium, set to take questions from a room crowded with reporters. From off camera came a rude, insistent voice. As the cameras turned to the questioner, they revealed Jorge Ramos, the pro–illegal immigration activist/anchor from the Spanish language Univision television network. This is the network that in pursuit of its racial agenda had already broken its TV contract with Trump over his comments opposing illegal immigration. Ironically, Univision seems obsessed with illegal immigration to the U.S., not to Mexico, where it carries penalties. The exchange went like this:

TRUMP: Okay, who is next? Yeah, please.

RAMOS: Mr. Trump, I have—

TRUMP: Excuse me. Sit down. You weren't called.

RAMOS: I have the right to ask the question.

TRUMP: Go back to Univision.

RAMOS: No.

Ramos persists, and suddenly, with a nod from Trump, a security official walks over and ushers a still-protesting Ramos out of the room. Eventually he is allowed back in and he has a five-minute debate with Trump over illegal immigration.

The event shocked the sensibilities of the mainstream press, which instinctively bends the knee to purveyors of racial grievances—especially when it is a fellow journalist. But many Americans loved Trump's refusal to tolerate Ramos's grandstanding and politicking badly disguised as journalism. Predictably, the press focused less on Ramos's conduct than it did on his ethnicity. Ramos is a Mexican-American. After the event, in an interview with the *Washington Post*, Ramos said pointedly, "Clearly, Mr. Trump's problem is with Latinos."

The *Post* reporter asked if Ramos was "saying Trump is racist or xenophobic." Ramos replied: "I don't like to put labels on anyone," though of course he just had. He went on, "I'm a reporter. I'd rather observe and describe and question." But Ramos was not observing, describing, and questioning, he was acting as an advocate—and as a protestor, trying to shout his way on camera.

It has become something of a joke, because of its ubiquity, for the Left to hurl accusations of racism. It is, for them, the shortest way to try to completely discredit and shut up their opponents. And the charge has been hurled so often, and so ridiculously at Trump that it has become a national joke. When The Donald was scheduled to host NBC's *Saturday Night Live*, a leftist group calling itself "Deport Racism" offered $5,000 for anyone in the audience to stand up during the live show and yell, "Trump's a racist." The *Saturday Night Live* crew, no dummies, and with Trump's eager participation, scheduled comedian Larry David to "interrupt" Trump by yelling, "Trump's a racist." The audience exploded in laughter when they realized who had yelled out the requested phrase, and when David said he wanted the 5,000 bucks.

Nevertheless, the accusations continue because the Left and other Trump critics have few reasonable arguments against a man who tells the truth. Shamefully, some Establishment Republicans, who embrace the poison of so-called "identity politics" and live in fear of losing "the

Hispanic vote" and other minority voters, have joined the left-wing media in asserting that Trump is a racist, because he believes in deporting *illegal* immigrants and because he frankly says that radical Islamic *terrorism* is a problem.

The fact is, we all *know* that radical Islam is a problem even if we're not allowed to say it. If the horrific murders in San Bernardino by radical Islamists don't illustrate this after years of similar attacks around the world, nothing will. We all *know*, if we think about it, that Hispanic Americans are not uniform in their political opinions or in their backgrounds. Why would they be? If one doesn't judge by skin color as the Left demands, Hispanics will be seen as—gasp!—human beings like every other human being on planet earth. We all *know*, again if we think about it, that illegal immigrants take jobs that might otherwise go to American citizens at the bottom of the income scale—including blacks and Hispanic Americans. We all *know*, if we're not politically indoctrinated with the racial politics of the Left, that *all* Americans suffer from crimes committed by illegal immigrants, who, gallingly and obviously, shouldn't be here in the first place, who should, by law, have been deported. Had Pedro Espinoza and Francisco Sanchez not been in

America, Jamiel Shaw Jr. and Kate Steinle would still be alive.

Jeb Bush put Establishment Republican cravenness into words when he criticized Trump's border control plan by saying, "They're doing high fives in the Clinton campaign right now when they're hearing this."

Of Trump's plans to crackdown on the threat of Islamist terror by better surveillance of Muslim populations in the United States, Bush called it "abhorrent" and John Kasich called it an attempt to "divide people." Kasich even authorized an ad that compared Trump to Hitler—citing, among other things, Trump's contretemps with Ramos as an alleged attempt to "suppress journalists." This was so over the top that *Washington Post* columnist Marc Thiessen, not a Trump fan, felt compelled to point out that "Kasich's ad achieves a political trifecta: It is offensive, inaccurate, and ineffective."

There is a pronounced inability—make that a refusal—to focus on just who are the real racists in America's midst. It is certainly not Donald Trump. It is certainly not his supporters who believe in colorblind enforcement of our laws. It is certainly not people who believe our immigration laws should be enforced. It is certainly not people who believe that good borders—like good fences—make good neighbors. It is certainly not people who, like Theodore Roosevelt, disdain the whole idea of a hyphenated American.

No, it is the Left that believes in a political strategy of racial division. Unfortunately, there are innumerable suicidal Republicans, intimidated by the Left and its accusations of racism, who are quite willing to endlessly concede the moral high ground to the Left and work toward the Left's objectives, only less radically, less expensively, and in a calmer tone of voice.

The Republican Party has a history of which it should be proud, but about which it seems to be ignorant. The Republican Party was founded as an anti-slavery party (and incidentally a pro–traditional marriage party against Mormon polygamy). For its entire history it has taken the stand that all men are created equal and endowed by their creator with certain unalienable rights. It has constantly supported colorblindness in American law. You will find no Republican disagreeing with John F. Kennedy's statement that "race has no place in American life or law." But nearly every Democrat is wedded to the notion that race should have a central place in American life and law.

And it has always been so. In what might seem the distant past, the Democrat Party was the party of slavery and segregation and "Jim Crow." The Democrats merely moved from trying to exclude Southern blacks from the political process for the party's political gain, to pandering to every ethnic and racial (and other) group for political gain. The formula is always the same—exploit race to push the progressive agenda.

Trump's opposition to *illegal* immigration is hardly racist, a classic case of projection from the Left that has built its entire history on racial politics. Trump's illegal immigration policies have nothing whatsoever to do with skin color. They have everything to do with putting the interests of American citizens first. The Democrats, however, are obsessed with race as a means to power. For them, illegal immigration has little to do with America's economy or security and everything to do with increasing the number of non-white voters who they assume will vote Democrat. And to that end, not only do the Democrats advocate for essentially open borders, they actively pursue policies that highlight racial differences; they don't look to assimilate immigrants to America, they look to assimilate America to immigrant voting blocs that the Democrats think they can control as long as Democrats can pander to race.

Most Americans naturally believe that America should *not* have immigration policies that endanger our nation's security. They want no more Tashfeen Maliks mass murdering Americans at an office Christmas party in the name of radical Islam. But the Democrat Party, which has barely acknowledged the plight of Christians in the Middle East and elsewhere in the world, targeted by Muslim radicals, believes in throwing open the door for Muslim "refugees" and has predictably implied that Donald Trump was a racist for warning that Syrian immigrants coming to the United States might include ISIS terrorists. Trump's warning was, inarguably, a statement of fact as even some members of the administration had to concede that it was impossible to impose thorough background checks on every alleged refugee. But to the Democrat Party, the potential gain in voters—not just the refugees and immigrants, but the much larger domestic constituencies that it was assumed would respond to the playing of the race card against the Republicans—outweighed any terrorist risk.

More than any other political figure, Donald Trump has stood against the Left's catcalls of racism and its silencing tactic of political correctness. Where all too many Republicans have knuckled under, Trump stands a figure

apart. His direct, frank approach—however unsophisti-
cated it might seem to his opponents who revel in a faux
sophistication and outright snobbery to average Americans—seems an expression of his direct, frank patriotism,
untrammeled by fear of the Left.

James Kalb explored this in a lengthy piece for
Chronicles magazine titled "Trump and the Culture of
Political Correctness." Kalb wrote:

> So he's not for sale, part of the club, or suscep-
> tible to pressure, and today that counts for
> everything. To put it differently, he seems his
> own man, and he's not politically correct. That
> matters, not just as a selling point, but substan-
> tively, because p.c. is a serious matter. At first
> people thought it a joke, then an annoyance,
> and eventually a constant drag on life in gen-
> eral. Now, in the age of flash mobs that enforce
> insane beliefs by destroying careers, people are
> realizing that p.c. is much more than that.
>
> In fact, political correctness is a genuine
> threat to any tolerable way of life. It's part of an
> attempt to...replace politics by an administrative

structure supposedly manned by infinitely capable and well-informed functionaries able to force reality to conform to the evolving open-ended demands of liberal theory.

In other words, p.c. is Totalitarianism 2.0: a bureaucratic system, seemingly gentle, that possesses unlimited power.... The attempt will fail, just as Bolshevism and Maoism failed, but it will do immense damage before it is given up.

...Domination of public life by p.c. elites has thus made it impossible for ordinary people to assert their complaints publicly in an acceptable way, so their objections can easily be shrugged off as the outbursts of ignorant bigots who will, in any event, soon become demographically irrelevant.

Who but Donald Trump has shown the guts and—most important—*the ability* to successfully withstand the blast furnace of the Left's politically correct tyranny? This is what makes Trump such a hero to his supporters; and it is why he is such a threat—in a way that no other Republican can match—to the Left. The Left might attack Trump and mock him, but it loses no sleep over the likes of Jeb Bush and John Kasich and the rest of the Republican field, whom the Democrats see as either beatable or easily co-opted. Donald Trump—because of his courage, his celebrity, and his independence—could break the grip of the Democrats' racial politics, winning voters that other Republicans can't reach or would never motivate. And Donald Trump, if elected president, would kowtow to no leftist piety. His very election would be a victory for liberty, a blow against the Left's stifling political correctness, its innate racism—and the first step to making America great again.

America Needs a Debt-Bomb Defuser

If we have another three or four years…we're at $18 trillion now—we're soon going to be at $20 trillion. According to the economists—who I'm not big believers in, but, nevertheless, this is what they're saying—that $24 trillion— we're very close—that's the point of no return. $24 trillion. We will be there soon. That's when we become Greece. That's when we become a country that's unsalvageable. And we're gonna be there very soon. We're gonna be there very soon.

—Donald Trump, announcing his presidential campaign, June 16, 2015

★   ★   ★

I n the aftermath of the 2008 financial crisis, Congress
created the Financial Crisis Inquiry Commission.
Among those serving on it was Peter J. Wallison, the
Arthur F. Burns Fellow in Financial Policy Studies at the
American Enterprise Institute and a former White House
Counsel to President Reagan. At the conclusion of the
Commission's work, Wallison charged that the Demo-
crats who ran the Commission had willfully ignored the
role that the federal government had played in creating
the worst financial disaster since the Great Depression.
Wrote Wallison in the *American Spectator*:

> George Santayana is often quoted for the aph-
> orism that "Those who cannot remember the
> past are condemned to repeat it." Looking back
> on the financial crisis, we can see why the study
> of history is often so contentious and why revi-
> sionist histories are so easy to construct. There
> are always many factors that could have caused
> a historical event; the difficult task is to discern
> which, among a welter of possible causes, were

the significant ones—the ones without which history would have been different.

Using this standard, I believe that the *sine qua non* of the financial crisis was U.S. government housing policy, which led to the creation of 27 million subprime and other risky loans— half of all mortgages in the United States— which were ready to default as soon as the massive 1997–2007 housing bubble began to deflate. If the U.S. government had not chosen this policy path—fostering the growth of a bubble of unprecedented size and an equally unprecedented number of weak and high-risk residential mortgages—the great financial crisis of 2008 would never have occurred.

New York Times Pulitzer Prize–winning reporter Gretchen Morgenson and co-author Joshua Rosner wrote *Reckless Endangerment: How Outsized Ambition, Greed and Corruption Led to Economic Armageddon*. The book was a searing examination of the role of the federal government in the financial catastrophe, in large part through the Federal National Mortgage Association (Fannie Mae), the Federal Home Loan Mortgage Corporation (Freddie Mac),

and the Clinton administration which had laid the ground-
work for the disaster, along with a cadre of lobbyists and
Washington insiders. Greed for money and power, under
a carapace of liberal good intentions (extending homeown-
ership to minority, low-income homebuyers), led all the
culpable participants to "ignore warning signs of imminent
disaster." Ironically, though the disaster happened on
George W. Bush's watch—and so he has been assigned
much of the blame—he was one of the few to warn, repeatedly, from 2001 to 2008, about the situation, demanding
reform of the system, only to be shouted down by the Left
as, you guessed it, a "racist."

The United States survived the crash, but millions of
Americans lost their homes, their jobs, their health insurance, and their savings. The next government-inflicted
meltdown could be even worse. "Our debt is a very dan-
gerous burden to carry around," wrote Trump in his
recent book *Crippled America: How to Make America
Great Again*. Indeed it is. And based on the performance
of the politicians who drove the nation into the last financial ditch, they have learned nothing. The debt keeps
growing and growing, with Barack Obama adding more
to the national debt than all forty-three of his predeces-
sors combined.

But it must be noted that President Obama is not the only problem. While he has been a spendthrift, Republicans have been his willing enablers. Senator Ted Cruz has even revealed in his book *A Time for Truth* that the Republican leadership was not only willing but eager to raise the debt limit for President Obama while holding a "show vote" that would give the party political cover. He wrote, "I heard more than one variation of 'That's what you say to folks back home [about not raising the debt limit]. You don't actually do it.' They were convinced they had a brilliant maneuver to increase our debt without any fingerprints."

According to Cruz, the GOP leadership was furious at someone (Ted Cruz) "with the temerity" to screw up their plan to deliberately mislead constituents about the GOP's commitment to maintain the debt ceiling and oppose Obama's reckless spending. Cruz, to his credit, is serious about reining in federal spending. It is one of many policies that he and Donald Trump share or on which they are in general agreement.

But the Republican Party as a whole has not, of late, been a party of fiscal responsibility. The Heritage Foundation has pointed out that President George W. Bush "presided over a $2.5 trillion increase in the public debt through 2008." That's nothing compared to Obama, but it's enormous in real terms, and certainly in terms of a party allegedly committed to fiscal restraint.

In short, Republicans generally talk a good game, but in practice, politicians in both parties would rather spend money on pet projects than practice the fiscal conservatism the country needs. In Great Britain Margaret Thatcher noticed the same problem with her Conservative Party— the Tories. Wrote Thatcher in her memoirs,

> At the level of principle, rhetorically and in opposition, it [the Conservative Party] opposed these [socialist] doctrines and preached the gospel of free enterprise with very little qualification.... But in the fine print of policy, especially in government, the Tory Party merely pitched camp in the long march to the left.... The result of this style of accommodationist politics...was...a "socialist ratchet" in which the British Labor governments moved Britain left, while a Tory government might loosen the corset of socialism...they never removed it.

Exactly. In American terms today, neither party seems prepared to deal seriously with the debt bomb.

Trump understands that not only can't the current $18.7 trillion debt bomb be endlessly kicked down the road (before it explodes), but that the first step to defusing it is with a tax plan that will encourage economic growth. Trump's tax plan, as the *Wall Street Journal* headlined, would "cut taxes for millions." That's just welcome news to the average taxpayer, but it is actually better than that. Trump's tax cuts are specifically directed at encouraging businesses to create new jobs. Former Reagan aide, economist, and CNBC anchor Larry Kudlow enthused on Steve Malzberg's *Newsmax* show about the Trump plan to cut the corporate tax rate to 15 percent:

> I really like Trump's plan. One of the things I just love about it is the 15 percent corporate tax rate.
>
> Remember, China's is 25, so if you want to beat China, lower the corporate tax rate—and that's just what Donald Trump has done. And by the way, small businesses...would pay the same low 15 percent rate. That's one of the key features.
>
> And, by the way, cutting into corporate tax is huge for economic growth. It'll give us a

gigantic advantage. Bring capital and businesses to the U.S., make us the most hospitable
place to invest—and that's what Donald Trump
has done.

There is more involved here than economic growth,
as crucial as that is. And there is more involved than rolling back the massive overregulation of the economy, as
important as that is. And there is even more than the
endless job of cutting the mindboggling "waste, fraud,
and abuse" in government programs, as vital as that is.

Trump is the one candidate with the commitment
and the personal standing to address the debt crisis. He
knows how Washington works—the whole system of
patronage and power and lobbyists. But he's an outsider
beholden to no one and no special interests. This makes
him virtually unique.

Make no mistake; it will take a political outsider to
fix the mess we're in financially. The political Establishment in Washington is too wedded to the status quo.
Peter Wallison, again writing in the *American Spectator*,
noted that not only had the federal government created
the 2008 financial crisis, but "The fact is that neither
political party, and no administration, is blameless;

the honest answer…is that government policy over many years caused the problem. The regulators, in both the Clinton and Bush administrations, were the enforcers of the reduced lending standards that were essential to the growth in home ownership and the housing bubble."

Ted Cruz calls this the "Washington Cartel" at work. He defined it this way in a speech to The Heritage Foundation: "What's happening in Washington is no accident. It is a concerted effort by corporate lobbyists and establishment politicians. Lobbyists and career politicians make up the Washington Cartel. Let me explain to you how it works: A bill is set to come before Congress, and career politicians' ears and wallets are open to the highest bidder. Corrupt backroom deals result in one interest group getting preferences over the other, although you give the other a chance to outbid them." And sometimes, "a very small interest group" gets "special carve-outs at the expense of taxpayers."

The Washington Cartel won't cut the fuse on the debt bomb. The bomb might go off and destroy the American economy, but the Washington Cartel would still prosper, and even profit from it. Washington, D.C., has become the one recession-proof part of America—because the Cartel has, in essence, constant access to your bank account (through taxes) and can even take out loans on your savings (through deficit spending), leaving you holding all the risk.

Donald Trump understands the system—but he is no longer a part of it. In a CNN interview with Anderson Cooper, Trump was asked about his view of Washington politicians and lobbyists. He replied: "Politicians are never going to turn this country around. Our country is a mess. The politicians are going to destroy this country. They're weak and they're ineffective. And they're controlled by the lobbyists and the special interests."

Cooper asked about Trump's understanding of the Washington system, and the conversation went this way:

> COOPER: Don't you have lobbyists, though?
>
> TRUMP: Absolutely. I have had lobbyists, and I have had some very good ones. They could do anything. They can take a politician and have him jump off this ledge.
>
> COOPER: Can you actually change that culture of corruption?
>
> TRUMP: Well, you can, in the sense that the top person can't be bought. I'm worth far too much money. I don't need anybody's

money. I'm not running with anybody's
money. I'm spending my own money. But
the lobbyists have—they totally control
these politicians. Just take a look. In one of
the articles very recently, I see [Jeb] Bush
with the lobbyists. And he's sitting there
with all of these people. They're totally telling him what to do, like a little puppet, and
the same with Hillary, and the same with
everybody else.

Donald Trump might seem a man apart, but there is a
precedent for putting someone like Trump in a position to
make dramatic and needed change in the financial system.

In 1934, with the nation still reeling from the Great
Depression, Franklin Roosevelt created the Securities and
Exchange Commission to be a Wall Street watchdog. He
selected as its first chairman Joseph P. Kennedy, the
father of future president John F. Kennedy. FDR's own
liberal allies were outraged at the appointment. They
thought that Kennedy was the last person to be put in
charge of the SEC because he had made a fortune as a
Wall Street speculator. The liberal *New Republic* called
the appointment "grotesque." FDR's own Secretary of

the Interior, the leftist Harold Ickes, growled to his diary: "The President has great confidence in him [Kennedy] because he has made his pile...and knows all the tricks of the trade. Apparently he is going on the assumption that Kennedy would now like to make a name for himself for the sake of his family, but I have never known many of these cases to work out as expected."

Yet as Kennedy's critics would later concede, the appointment of the man who "knew the tricks of the trade" on Wall Street turned out to be a smashing success. Biographer Richard Whalen records that when Kennedy departed from the SEC:

> ...many early critics had come to regard the SEC as the New Deal's most constructive reform.... His [Kennedy's] accomplishment was unmistakable. He had taken a law that seemed almost unworkable, and had administered it so as to reassure business, simplify corporate borrowing, and boost investor confidence. To his successor as SEC chairman.... he turned over an experiment that had achieved the stature of an institution in the amazingly brief period of four hundred and thirty one days.

There is no reason to believe that Donald Trump could not enjoy similar success in defusing the debt bomb—a bomb that, to date, no politician has dealt with effectively. Donald Trump understands economics. He knows how Washington works. But unlike the Washington Cartel, he has nothing to gain from the deficit spending and the system as it is. He is perfectly placed to prevent an economic catastrophe that likely no other politician has the courage, the independence, and the competence to handle.

Who better qualified to charge in to a Washington infested with special interest lobbyists and insiders like those who caused the 2008 financial crisis and head off the looming explosion of the debt bomb than Donald Trump?

America Needs a Leader Who Can Get Things Done

Some people see things as they are and say why.
I dream things that never were and say why not.

—Senator Robert F. Kennedy quoting George Bernard Shaw

★   ★   ★

President George Herbert Walker Bush confessed he was never very good on the "vision thing," which might explain why, nice as he was, he was a one-term president.

Successful presidents need a vision of where they want to take the country. They need to be able to communicate that vision, especially in the media-intensive world in which we live.

But most of all, they need to be strong executives, leaders who know how to get things done.

When we think of great presidents, we think of great accomplishments: Lincoln restoring the Union and ending slavery; Franklin Roosevelt bringing hope after the Great Depression and winning the Second World War; Ronald Reagan reviving America's spirits and economy after the Jimmy Carter "malaise" and "stagflation," and winning the Cold War.

It is wrong to think that the challenges America faces today require anything less than a great leader to meet them. Our nation's borders are uncontrolled. Our country is threatened by radical Islamic terrorism and the

restive power of China. It is a commonplace among foreign policy analysts that our foreign policy is adrift; that
we have no international strategy worthy of the name.

Domestically, America's economy remains in dire
straits. Un-American pessimism about the future is set-
tling over the land just as it was in Jimmy Carter's day.
America seems more divided and at odds with itself than
at any time since the riots of the late 1960s.

Americans are craving a leader who will set a new
course and, to coin a phrase, make America great again.

The first step to doing that is creating more American
jobs, and in poll after poll, by overwhelming percentages
(as much as 30 points), Americans say that they believe
Donald Trump is the best qualified candidate to create
private sector jobs, which makes sense, because what else
has Donald Trump done his entire life but build businesses and create jobs (something incidentally that his
political critics can't claim for themselves). How many
jobs has Donald Trump created over the years? I asked
him directly in a May 2014 interview for the *American
Spectator* and he responded:

Oh, tens of thousands. Even now, I mean, in
four weeks I start work on Pennsylvania Avenue

in Washington, D.C., right between the Capitol and the White House. Right smack in the best location, the old Post Office. And we're creating tremendous numbers of jobs. We're basically rebuilding it as one of the great hotels of the world. See, there's a thing you couldn't do without tremendous incentives. You know it's a very expensive project. A lot of people are going to be employed, a lot of jobs created. And as you know, I'm in the process of—pretty close to—finishing up at Trump National Doral, eight-hundred acres right in the middle of Miami. So you know, I mean, we have tremendous jobs, we have jobs going up all over the world.

A CNN poll in August 2015 showed 45 percent of Republicans chose Trump as the candidate best able to handle the economy. His closest competitor was Jeb Bush at 8 percent. The same poll showed that Trump was trusted by 44 percent as best equipped to handle illegal immigration, Bush again his closest competitor at 12 percent. Likewise, when the question shifted to who would best be able to handle ISIS, Trump won at 32 percent, double the number of his then-closest competitor Bush.

Why is this? A November 19, 2015, Bloomberg poll provided one answer, with a resounding 73 percent saying Trump was the Republican candidate for president who "knows the most about how to get things done." J. Ann Selzer, whose Iowa-based Selzer & Co. conducted the poll, surmised: "Trump's greatest strength has always been what people think he can do."

Getting things done is what Donald Trump does. No other candidate can match his accomplishments as an executive. In 1983, *Town and Country* magazine profiled Donald Trump, a then-thirty-seven-year-old aspiring mogul, and concluded, "Show Trump an obstacle and he's ready in an instant to hurdle it; give him a 'no' and he'll rack his brain to find a way to get a 'yes.' Even in normal conversation, he will frequently interrupt the other person with an 'Okay, I understand' as soon as he's grasped the gist of what he or she is saying, and then move briskly on to the next topic."

His manner: brisk, because time is money. His reaction to opposition: overcome it. Throughout his business career, Donald Trump has surmounted the odds and beat the regulators and the naysayers and the lawyers and media and the politicians and the sideline critics who kept telling him that projects he wanted to pursue couldn't be done.

Trump got them done, creating the jobs that went with them.

In one of many examples of his persistence and success, *Town and Country* recounted how

> back in 1976, when Donald Trump first proposed to buy, gut, and then completely remodel New York's dilapidated Commodore Hotel on East 42nd Street, most dispassionate observers, and some passionate ones, thought he should have his head examined. For the last six years of its life, the Commodore Hotel had lost $1.5 million per annum, and contributed not a penny to the city's tax coffers. The overall hotel-occupancy rate in New York had slipped to an abysmal 69 percent, and the city as a whole was teetering on its own financial tightrope. Donald's father, veteran real estate developer Fred C. Trump, recalls telling his son, "This is like trying to buy a ticket on the Titanic." But Donald, only 30 years old at the time, was not to be dissuaded from the project.
>
> "Forty-Second Street back then was not looking so good," he admits in his carefully

modulated tones. "The Chrysler Building had just defaulted on its mortgage; there was a flea market operating on the corner of Park Avenue. A lot of people were predicting that East 42nd Street was going to go the way of West 42nd Street. But one day I walked down to Grand Central Station, right next door to the block the Commodore sat on, and I watched the thousands of people streaming in and out, and I thought to myself, 'How can this be a bad deal?' And that turned out to be correct thinking, I guess."

Donald's "correct thinking" resulted in the showy, and hugely successful, Grand Hyatt Hotel, the largest new hotel to be built in New York since the Hilton, some twenty years before.

When Donald Trump talks about "making America great again," it is no empty rhetoric, no idle boast. Donald Trump was one of the developers who helped make New York City great again after a period of decline and decay.

The building of the iconic Trump Tower is a perfect illustration of Trump's vision and can-do style. Where other would-be developers had been stymied, the young Donald

Trump hurdled one challenge after another—from buying the property itself (one of the choicest in the world as it adjoins Tiffany's on Fifth Avenue), to getting everything from the credit at Chase Manhattan Bank, a building partner (the Equitable Life Assurance Society), clearances from the city (obtained after winning a court battle), and air rights. A last minute hurdle came when preservationists objected that the sculptures on the existing Bonwit Teller building on the property be saved. Trump would have none of it, and gave the order to his construction crew to get on with the demolition—*now*. And Trump got it done. It was a bravura performance that benefited not only Trump but the people of New York.

Another famous "Trump gets it done" story involves his saving of New York City's Wollman Skating Rink. In an August 2015 *Forbes* article titled "Donald Trump and the Wollman Rinking of American Politics," writers Irwin Kula and Craig Hatkoff summarized the tale:

> The Wollman Rink incident underscores the fascinating impact that Donald Trump is making on the political landscape and the American psyche irrespective of the outcome of the presidential campaign. Wollman Skating Rink today

is one of the most iconic amenities for New Yorkers and tourists located in Central Park just a stone's throw north of the Plaza Hotel (which was once owned by Donald Trump).

Having fallen into utter disrepair during the New York City fiscal crisis, unable to make ice, the city's Parks Department embarked on a total refurbishment of the facility in 1980, estimating it would take two years to complete. After six years and having flushed $13 million down the drain, the city announced they would have to start all over again and it would take another two years to complete. Wollman Rink had quite visibly failed. The Wollman Rink fiasco amplified the public perception of the general incompetence of government and their inability to complete even the simplest projects.

Enter the Donald. In late May of 1986 the 39-year-old Trump made an offer to Mayor Ed Koch. Trump would step in and take over the construction and operation of the project for no profit and have it up and running in time for the holiday season.... A very public Trump-Koch feud ensued; Donald ultimately prevailed taking on the responsibility to finish the rink in less than six months for no more than $3 million. The city politicos could only hope that when Donald failed it would divert attention from their own incompetence.

Instead of failing, Trump finished the job in just four months at a final cost 25 percent below the budget. It wasn't rocket science according Trump [*sic*]. It was common sense and "management."

The Trump life story is littered with these "can do" moments. They stand in stark contrast to the feeble inability of Republicans to get anything done, when it comes to their campaign promises, let alone to the general spendthrift incompetence of federal agencies and departments. One of the prerequisites of a presidential campaign is the candidate touting his or her "accomplishments." Talk show host Sean Hannity has made a game of asking the Hillary supporters who call in to his radio show to name one Hillary accomplishment. To the tune of game show music, silence if not bafflement ensues. Such is not so with Trump accomplishments. They are everywhere.

The Trump Organization that Trump built step by step beginning in New York City is filled to overflowing with projects listed in real estate, hotels, golf courses, international realty, entertainment and television, books and merchandise. From New York to Hawaii, Trump real estate projects alone can be found in nine American cities, as well as abroad on four continents—in Turkey, Panama, South Korea, Canada, the Philippines, India, Uruguay, and Brazil.

Trump merchandise runs the gamut from home furniture to cufflinks. His golf courses are scattered from America to Dubai. His books have been *New York Times* bestsellers and his television shows have been among the most popular. Like all businessmen he has setbacks as well as successes, but his $10 billion empire is no small accomplishment.

Can that business success translate into political success? The answer is yes, and not because business and politics and government are the same (they're not) but because Trump has the kind of leadership that I saw in President Ronald Reagan when I worked for him. Reagan had a sign on his Oval Office desk that read: "It CAN be done." Reagan had no time for naysayers, and neither does Trump.

Every human soul is unique, and I'm not saying that Donald Trump is Ronald Reagan. But like Reagan, Trump is a man of vision, a patriot who finds his country in despair and disarray and wants to make it great again. And like Reagan, Trump is not just a visionary, a man of optimism and faith; he is a man who can get things done. Politically, he's already gotten things done by utterly changing the terms of political debate. Single-handedly, Trump has ignited a serious debate over illegal immigration, the treatment of veterans by the grossly negligent Veterans Administration, and the Obama administration's utter lack of a coherent and effective strategy against ISIS and radical Islam. He has also refused to be silenced or intimidated by the enforcers of political correctness and identity politics and by an almost uniformly hostile media.

Ronald Reagan took heat when he called the Soviet Union an "evil empire"—but he was entirely correct. Ronald Reagan's own State Department and National Security Council staff were terrified at what the reaction might be when he delivered his now-famous speech at the Berlin Wall where he challenged the Soviet leader Mikhail Gorbachev, saying the now iconic line "Mr. Gorbachev, tear down this wall!" His strategy to win the Cold War was Trumpian in its simplicity, "We win, they lose."

That kind of simplicity grates on liberals and the Republican Establishment who all too often take the position that their job is to manage American decline and defeat, to help reconcile the American people to lower economic expectations and a declining presence in the world, to ever more taxing and spending because almost every politician's "accomplishments" are based on spending more taxpayer dollars, to leaving our borders undefended because business wants cheap labor and Democrats want to import what they assume will be Democrat voters.

But Donald Trump is different. When it comes to ISIS, his strategy is Reagan's, "We win, they lose." When it comes to the border, he believes in a simple solution: how about enforcing the law against *illegal* immigration and coming up with a better system of legal immigration—one that can prevent the next San Bernardino? When it comes to political correctness, he says, why not tell the truth? When it comes to the economy and trade: why not put American workers first and why not encourage businesses to create more jobs by cutting their tax rates so that they have more money to invest? Simple ideas, but good ones—and ones that we can have confidence that he, unlike most any other candidate, will actually be able to execute, because Trump gets things done.

America Needs a President Who Puts America First

Donald Trump on ISIS: He *"would hit them so hard and so fast that they wouldn't know what happened."*
—Conservative Political Action Conference, 2015

Donald Trump on Iraq: I said it very strongly, years ago . . . I love the military, and I want to have the strongest military that we've ever had, and we need it more now than ever. But I said, "Don't hit Iraq," because you're going to totally destabilize the Middle East. Iran is going to take over the Middle East, Iran and somebody else will get the oil, and it turned out that Iran is now taking over Iraq. Think of it. Iran is taking over Iraq, and they're taking it over big league.

We spent $2 trillion in Iraq, $2 trillion. We lost thousands of lives, thousands in Iraq. We have wounded soldiers… all over the place, thousands and thousands of wounded soldiers. And we have nothing. We can't even go there. We have nothing. And every time we give Iraq equipment, the first time a bullet goes off in the air, they leave it. Last week, I read 2,300 Humvees—these are big vehicles— were left behind for the enemy.... 2,300 sophisticated vehicles, they ran, and the enemy took them.

—Donald Trump, announcing his presidential campaign, June 16, 2015

★   ★   ★

I n *The Art of War*, Sun Tzu, the great Chinese general and strategist, wrote, "Therefore the clever combatant imposes his will on the enemy, but does not allow the enemy's will to be imposed on him."

On the morning of November 13, 2015, Donald Trump was discussing ISIS and what he saw as the completely ineffectual response of the Obama administration in fighting an enemy that glories in cutting off children's heads and crucifying opponents. Trump said, "ISIS is making a tremendous amount of money because they have certain oil camps, certain areas of oil that they took away." He continued, "They have some in Syria, some in Iraq. I would bomb the s--- out of 'em. I would just bomb those suckers. That's right. I'd blow up the pipes.... I'd blow up every single inch. There would be nothing left. And you know what, you'll get Exxon to come in there and in two months, you ever see these guys, how good they are, the great oil companies? They'll rebuild that sucker, brand new—it'll be beautiful." And instead of pumping oil for ISIS, it would be pumping oil for the West.

Mere hours later, ISIS terrorists—the "JV team" as President Obama once scorned them—brought hell to

Paris, in multiple terrorist attacks that left 130 dead and more than 350 wounded. While France responded with a promise of retaliation, and cooperation with the Russians against ISIS, Obama was cool to French pleas that the United States and Russia cooperate to fight radical Islam in the Middle East. Throughout the course of his administration he has seen himself as the great reconciler of Islam and the West; and when radical Islam doesn't cooperate he seems unenthusiastic about doing anything more than, as one White House adviser once put it, "leading from behind."

As this is written, ISIS terrorists have physical bases in Iraq, Syria, and Libya—all of this on Obama's watch; and his former secretary of state Hillary Rodham Clinton shares a good part of the blame too. Libyan policy was left largely to her by the president. It was she who called the American-assisted toppling of Muammar Gaddafi—a dictator but one who had tried to make amends with the West after the U.S.-led invasion of Iraq—"smart power at its best." It hasn't turned out so "smart," with Libya in chaos and a haven for Islamist terrorists. Is it any wonder Trump labels Hillary the "worst Secretary of State in the history of the United States"?

Donald Trump's business success is based on many talents, but one of the most important is his quick ability to read other people; he has good instincts. In *The Art of the Deal* he noted that deal-making was "mostly about instincts. You can take the smartest kid at Wharton, the one who gets straight A's and has a 170 IQ, and if he doesn't have the instincts, he'll never be a successful entrepreneur."

Or a successful president of the United States, either.

In 2000, Donald Trump made a startling prediction in his book *The America We Deserve*:

> I really am convinced we're in danger of the sort of terrorist attacks that will make the bombing of the Trade Center look like kids playing with firecrackers. No sensible analyst rejects this possibility, and plenty of them, like me, are not wondering if but when it will happen.
>
> One day we're told that a shadowy figure with no fixed address named Osama bin-Laden is public enemy number one, and U.S. jetfighters lay waste to his camp in Afghanistan. He escapes back under some rock, and a

few news cycles later it's on to a new enemy
and new crisis.

Donald Trump apparently had better instincts on the
terrorist threat than almost anyone in the American
government.

In March 2003, as the U.S. invasion of Iraq was getting under way, Trump was in Hollywood making the
rounds of post-Oscar parties. The *Washington Post*
caught up with him and wrote this:

> Donald Trump, with Amazonian beauty Mela-
> nia Knauss at his side, pronounces on the war
> and the stock market: "If they keep fighting it
> the way they did today, they're going to have a
> real problem."
>
> Looking as pensive as a "Nightline" talking
> head, the Donald concludes, "The war's a
> mess," before sweeping off into the crowd.

In July 2004, a Reuters headline declared, "Donald
Trump Would 'Fire' Bush Over Iraq Invasion." Reuters
quoted Trump as saying: "Look at the war in Iraq and
the mess that we're in. I would never have handled it that

way. Does anybody really believe that Iraq is going to be a wonderful democracy where people are going to run down to the voting box and gently put in their ballot and the winner is happily going to step up to lead the country?" That was a clearer-eyed analysis than what governed the Bush administration and its wise men with their decades of experience in Washington.

Trump went on, "C'mon. Two minutes after we leave, there's going to be a revolution, and the meanest, toughest, smartest, most vicious guy will take over. And he'll have weapons of mass destruction, which Saddam didn't have."

Trump said of the Iraq invasion, "What was the purpose of the whole thing? Hundreds and hundreds of young people killed. And what about the people coming back with no arms and no legs? Not to mention the other side. All those Iraqi kids who've been blown to pieces. And it turns out that all of the reasons for the war were blatantly wrong. All this for nothing!"

Did his opposition to the Iraq war mean that Trump was weak on fighting international terrorism? On the contrary, Trump asserted that if he were president the United States would be waging a much more aggressive, but targeted, strategic, and effective war on terrorism— not going to war against a secular dictator like Saddam

Hussein, but concentrating on eliminating the leaders of Islamic terrorism. He said that under a Trump administration, "Bin Laden would have been caught long ago. Tell me, how is it possible that we can't find a guy who's six-foot-six and supposedly needs a dialysis machine? Can you explain that one to me? We have all our energies focused on one place [Iraq], where they shouldn't be focused." For Trump it was, again, a question of management, of setting priorities, and of knowing what needed to get done and doing it, not being distracted by irrelevancies. The instincts that have made him one of the world's most successful businessmen could also make him one of our more effective recent commanders in chief, the most effective since, well, perhaps Ronald Reagan.

Trump's vision of America's role in the world is, after all, decidedly Reaganesque. He believes in Reagan's "peace through strength." When it comes to negotiating, he believes, as Reagan did with the Soviets, in the doctrine of "trust, but verify." He believes, like Reagan, that rolling back tyranny requires a strong military, but does not necessarily require war.

In his eight years in the White House, Reagan invaded exactly one country—the island nation of Grenada. He did so to prevent Grenada, which had just suffered a Communist coup, from being remade as a military base for Communist expansion in Central and Latin America. The invasion was a rousing success.

But early in his administration, Reagan had signed on to one military intervention he later came to regret: sending U.S. peace-keeping troops to Lebanon as part of a U.S.-French Multinational Force. The American Marines stationed in Beirut were attacked in their barracks by an explosives-filled truck driven by a suicide bomber. The casualties: 243 dead Marines. Reagan was both angry and shaken. He would have to make the calls to the parents of each Marine, and he later recalled one anguished father asking him, "Are we in Lebanon for any reason worth my son's life?" Reagan says he gulped, but said yes.

But after the bombing of the Marine Barracks, Reagan instructed his national security team to adopt what he called "a set of principles to guide America in the application of military forces abroad." There were four, all of which seem equally to guide Donald Trump's thinking about maintaining a strong defense and using our military forces wisely. Reagan listed the four principles in his memoirs as follows:

1. The United States should not commit its forces to military action overseas unless the cause is vital to our national interest.

2. If the decision is made to commit our forces to combat abroad, it must be done with the clear intent and support to win. It should not be a halfway or tentative commitment, and there must be clearly defined and realistic objectives.

3. Before we commit our troops to combat, there must be reasonable assurance that the cause we are fighting for and the actions we take will have the support of the American people and Congress. (We all felt that the Vietnam War had turned into such a tragedy because military action had been undertaken without sufficient assurances that the American people were behind it.)

4. Even after all these other tests were met, our troops should be committed to combat abroad only as a last resort, when no other choice is available.

Trump's similar foreign policy principles were out-lined in his 2011 book *Time to Get Tough*. Wrote Trump:

> I believe that any credible American foreign policy doctrine should be defined by at least seven core principles:
> 1. American interests come first. Always. No apologies.
> 2. Maximum firepower and military pre-paredness.
> 3. Only go to war to win.
> 4. Stay loyal to your friends and suspicious of your enemies.
> 5. Keep the technological sword razor sharp.
> 6. See the unseen. Prepare for threats before they materialize.
> 7. Respect and support our present and past warriors.

The key to America's success in the world, Trump believes, is leadership. But American leadership has fallen a long way from the days of Truman, Eisenhower, Kennedy,

Nixon, Ford, and Reagan. In fact, Trump is not afraid to say that American foreign policy under President Obama and Secretaries of State Hillary Clinton and John Kerry has been nothing short of "stupid." In my May 2014 interview for the *American Spectator*, I asked him directly about American leadership, to which he responded,

> They don't understand the challenge. And the challenge is only going to get worse, and China is two years ahead of schedule.
>
> Our leaders are impotent. They have no idea what's going on with respect to China—I can also say with respect to Russia, and virtually every other place on the planet. But China, what they have done economically is incredible. They have taken our jobs, they make our products, they have done so brilliantly for themselves and it's hard to believe we allow it to happen.
>
> We have all the cards. We built China. Because the money they've sucked out of this country has gone to build bridges and schools and roadways and everything, things that we don't have, that we can't build. And on top of it they then loan us money. So China is a huge problem and it's only

gotten worse. It's inconceivable that our leaders don't see the China problem in this country.

Trump knows, as a businessman, that American foreign policy is not just about war and peace; it's also about trade and jobs. Because he believes in putting American economic interests first, he has been accused of being a "protectionist," an anti–free trader. In his speech announcing his candidacy for the Republican nomination for president, he responded directly to this criticism:

> I'm a free trader. But the problem with free trade is you need really talented people to negotiate for you. If you don't have people that know business, not just a political hack that got the job because he made a contribution to a campaign, free trade is terrible.
>
> Free trade can be wonderful if you have smart people, but we have people that are stupid. We have people that are controlled by special interests. And it's just not going to work.

In his 2000 book, *The America We Deserve*, he wrote that "We need tougher negotiations, not protectionist walls around America. We need to ensure that foreign markets are as open to our products as our country is to theirs. Our long-term interests require that we cut better deals with our world trading partners."

This might seem like common sense, but it is incomprehensible to the Washington Establishment. The first Obama-appointed U.S. Trade Representative was Ron Kirk, a one-time Mayor of Dallas, Texas, an unsuccessful candidate for the U.S. Senate, and (maybe you guessed it) *a lobbyist*. He perfectly illustrated Trump's point that the men and women appointed to negotiate American trade deals are more often than not simply failed politicians, political cronies, and Washington insiders—not successful businessmen and expert negotiators. The North American Free Trade Agreement, which Trump has called a "disaster," was negotiated by President Clinton's Trade Representative Mickey Kantor, who—wait for it—had been a Los Angeles lawyer and a Democrat Party activist and fundraiser.

If you're Donald Trump and you see bad economic deals being negotiated by U.S. government trade representatives without backgrounds in business, and who have no idea of how to negotiate, no instinct for the art of the deal, it's no wonder that you might get angry on America's behalf—and it's no wonder that American voters, American workers, might respond to your message. The Washington Establishment likes to pretend that the issues of governance, of trade, of foreign and domestic policy, are too complex for the "simple" answers that Donald Trump likes to give. But Donald Trump has a familiar ally in Ronald Reagan. In his famous speech, "A Time for Choosing," Reagan declared, "They say the world has become too complex for simple answers. They are wrong. There are no easy answers, but there are simple answers."

Reagan and Trump have it right, much as it infuriates the media and Washington Establishment whose loathing of Trump is driven in large part because he makes a mockery of them.

But if the media pundits are so smart, how come they are so often wrong (including about Trump's enduring popularity)?

If the Washington Establishment is so smart, how come the country is in such a mess, with entitlement payments we can't afford, a debt bomb ticking to explode, an infrastructure crumbling to pieces despite federal spending of almost unbelievable proportions, an education system better at indoctrinating students in political correctness than in preparing them for the real world (or exposing them to real and challenging ideas), a foreign policy of retrenchment and retreat, and so many other problems that it seems nearly impossible that America could have fallen so far so fast from the heady days of the Reagan-Bush victory of the Cold War, when commentators were talking about America as the lone superpower in a "unipolar" world?

There's an entire school of philosophy centered on the idea of "Occam's Razor," which boiled down to layman's terms is that the simplest and most direct answer is the one most likely to be right. American decline is the direct result of bad leadership, which has come from Washington, and from leftist political correctness that has too long gone unchallenged.

For Trump, as for Reagan, putting America first puts everything else into perspective. It seems crazy that we have to look hard for a candidate who will truly put America first. But that's exactly what Donald Trump will do.

REASON SIX

America Needs a Rebuilder for the Republican Party

Ronald Reagan made it clear today that he intends to play a major role in rebuilding the Republican Party by courting conservatives who now call themselves Democrats and Independents.

—The *New York Times*, December 16, 1976

★　★　★

I t's time.

In fact, it's well past time for the Republican Party to open its doors once again as it did in the Reagan era. To welcome in those who agree with GOP principles be they Democrats, Independents, or Americans who have never before participated in the political system.

Donald Trump is doing exactly this, just as Ronald Reagan did before him. And, just as Reagan did, Trump has come under fire from the party's Establishment. If Reagan was an extremist, a cowboy, and an actor with no business running for president, Trump to his critics is also an extremist, a garish billionaire, and a reality TV star who similarly has no business running for president.

Here's what some in the Republican Establishment have said about Donald Trump:

Peter Wehner, a former aide to President George W. Bush, writing in the *New York Times*, called Donald Trump a demagogue "who delights in tearing down the last remaining guardrails in our political culture…. [I]t's up to my fellow Republican primary voters to repudiate his malignant candidacy. Not doing so would be a moral indictment of our party."

A different political analyst might say that losing the last two presidential elections is an electoral indictment of the party, and maybe something should change.

Karl Rove, another former aide to President George W. Bush, has called Donald Trump "a complete idiot." This, from the political "architect" of the George W. Bush presidential campaigns, the first of which produced victory by the grace of the United States Supreme Court and 537 Florida votes, the second with a narrow 118,000 vote margin in Ohio—the weakest showing for a reelected president since Woodrow Wilson in 1916.

Yet another George W. Bush White House aide, Michael Gerson, has said that "I know that the success of Trump would be the downfall of the GOP." Perhaps he missed the fact that the downfall of the GOP happened on the watch of George W. Bush, who was never able to produce Reaganesque landslides, much less, as Reagan also did, elect a Republican successor. Thus setting the country up for two terms of Barack Obama, by far the most left-wing president we've ever had.

Have we ever heard language like this from the Republican Establishment, knocking its leading presidential candidate? The answer is yes, we certainly have. The Republican Establishment felt almost exactly the same way about Ronald Reagan as they do about Donald Trump—and you don't have to take my word for it. Here's former president Gerald R. Ford, interviewed in the *New York Times* in March 1980:

> Asked if he shared the view that Mr. Reagan could not win, Mr. Ford said "It would be an impossible situation" because Mr. Reagan is "perceived as a most conservative Republican."
>
> "A very conservative Republican," he said, "can't win in a national election."
>
> Meaning that Mr. Reagan can't win?
>
> "That's right," Mr. Ford said.

Ford was a good man, but a decided Establishment, moderate Republican, like the Bushes—and for all his wildly off-base criticisms of Reagan as being unable to win, Ford himself never won a presidential election. In fact, he lost to the very candidate, Jimmy Carter, that Reagan crushed in 1980. Reagan went on to win a landslide reelection. When he left office he had an approval rating of nearly 70 percent. And as mentioned, Reagan's vice president, George Herbert Walker Bush, coasted into the presidency on the wave of the public's warm feelings for Ronald Reagan. But the Establishment-backed Bush could not win reelection himself; and his son, George W. Bush, whose aides are so vehemently anti-Trump, only squeaked by in two close elections, leaving the White House with an approval rating of 22 percent. So which is the better model for Republican candidates to follow—that of Reagan or of the Establishment Bushes and Ford?

It's another one of those simple answers the mandarins don't want to hear.

In fact, the electoral appeal of Trump is very similar to the electoral appeal of Reagan. After the Establishment Ford's 1976 loss to Carter, an exasperated Reagan sat down with the *New York Times* a month after the Ford defeat and made it plain that the key to a Republican success was throwing open the doors of the GOP and, as the *Times* wrote up the story, "courting conservatives who now call themselves Democrats and independents."

Trump is making an effort to broaden the reach of the party with both African Americans and blue collar workers, to Americans fed up with political correctness, to people who think that the Establishments of both parties have done a terrible job of managing the economy and conducting our foreign policy. Like Reagan he is appealing to Americans whose core beliefs are conservative, though their party registration might be Democrat or Independent.

The Bushes are wonderful people—full disclosure, I worked for Jack Kemp when he was Secretary of Housing and Urban Development in the administration of George Herbert Walker Bush—but as political leaders their record is not the best. It was Reagan, not the Bushes, who created a new Republican coalition that created a period of Republican dominance. It was the Bush brand of Establishment, "compassionate conservatism" that utterly "tainted the brand" of the GOP as a party that didn't have the courage of its alleged conservative convictions, raising taxes (in the case of George H. W. Bush) and spending like a drunken sailor (under George W. Bush), in both cases expanding rather than contracting the reach of the federal government.

Time and again Establishment, moderate Republicans insist that the only sure path to electoral success is to embrace slightly more moderate versions of the Democrats' policies. The Democrats and their liberal allies in the media set the tone in Washington, they set the parameters of debate, and the Republican Establishment plays by their rules and accepts many of their assumptions, whether it is that "compassion" means spending more taxpayer money, or that the federal government should play a greater role in our schools or in our economy (especially with federal support for so-called "green energy" programs), or that the Left has all the best arguments, in fact the only allowable arguments, on social and cultural questions. That it should go without saying, this is and has repeatedly been a recipe for Republican defeat. Losing "moderate" or Establishment Republicans produced nominees Hoover (1932), Landon (1936), Willkie (1940), Dewey (twice, in 1944 and 1948), Nixon (who ran as a moderate in 1960), Ford (1976), Bush 41 (1992), Dole (1996), McCain (2008), and Romney (2012). Suffice to say, time after time the American people have rejected the idea of a me-too party. Who needs a party that lacks convictions—that, in other words, can't be trusted? Contrary to the myth of moderates, no Republican was going to win in 1964 in the shocking aftermath of President Kennedy's assassination. Lyndon Johnson's—and liberalism's—popularity was at flood tide. Goldwater himself knew he would lose. But he began the process of defeating the Eastern GOP Establishment's control over the nominating process that had produced one presidential defeat after another. Two years after Goldwater's cleansing of the GOP Establishment stables, 1966 produced a GOP landslide, among other things electing Ronald Reagan governor of California in a million-vote victory. Interestingly if not surprisingly, the California GOP Establishment had spent all of 1965 and early 1966 insisting that Reagan was too extreme to ever be elected governor. That was wildly wrong as well.

Whatever one says of Trump, he's not a follower, he's a leader. He doesn't care what the Establishment says, he says what *he* thinks—and he believes what he says. To the American people, that's a breath of fresh air in a political atmosphere that's grown acrid and stale. And it is what has allowed Trump to appeal to voters outside of the Republican base (though he does very well there too).

When Donald Trump paid a visit to the blue collar town of Birch Run, Michigan, twenty minutes south of Flint, in August 2015, the *Washington Post*, no Trump cheerleader, headlined Trump's appearance this way: "Why Donald Trump makes sense to many voters—even some Democrats."

Post reporter David Weigel, who was on the scene in Flint and Birch Run, wrote,

> Trump's rise and persistence as a presidential candidate has been credited to name recognition, to voter anger and to a specific contempt

for the Republican Party establishment. But he is also the candidate talking most directly about the loss of manufacturing jobs to foreign countries.

…On Twitter, "Make America Great Again" is a goofy, meme-ready slogan, best displayed on ironic hats. There are places, such as Michigan, where it makes real sense.

That was on full display at a rollicking news conference and campaign rally where Trump again and again attacked "stupid" American leaders who were buffaloed by "cunning" Mexican and Chinese politicians.

What Weigel is describing here is the Trump version of what came to be known as "Reagan Democrats," who, just as Reagan predicted after Ford's defeat, swarmed into the GOP tent with Reagan's appeals to conservatives generally. As Weigel pointed out, "Flint and Saginaw, the cities south and north of Trump's speech on Tuesday, had voted for Democrats," and so has Michigan as a whole in every presidential election since 1992. But Trump's brand of tell-it-like-it-is economic populism, his unashamed belief that the interests of American workers should come first, potentially puts a state like Michigan in play for the Republicans in the 2016 presidential election—if the Republicans nominate Trump.

It was the conservative Republican Ronald Reagan who was endorsed by the Teamsters Union in 1984. Donald Trump is the Republican most likely to appeal to such blue collar workers in 2016—updating the Reagan Democrats to become twenty-first-century Trump Democrats. It is hard, if not impossible, to imagine any of the other leading Republican candidates as having a better message for, and a better rapport with, blue collar conservatives than the billionaire populist Donald Trump—and that could be electoral dynamite.

In December 2015, Trump's prowess as a job creator was one very important reason why he was endorsed by a group of black pastors in Virginia. One of those black pastors endorsing Trump was the Reverend Dr. Steve Parson, who after meeting with Trump made a point of saying this, as quoted by *Time* magazine,

> "People ask me, well why are you endorsing Donald Trump?" Parson said. "My opinion: he's the best, and the only one that can beat Hillary Clinton. We have to win. And one

thing about Donald Trump is he's a winner, Amen. He knows how to create wealth, can I get an Amen? And as a black minister…we're right in the inner city, and I'll tell you we need jobs, we need employment, we need businesses. And I tell you who better to help us help our- selves than Donald Trump?"

If creating jobs is the issue, Trump has the best—if not the only—private sector record. If the issue is con- necting with the American people in places like blue collar Michigan, Trump is the only leading Republican candidate who seems likely to succeed.

There are Republican strategists who think that America's demographics have changed so dramatically that the only way to elect a Republican president is to either nominate someone with a Hispanic name or a Hispanic spouse or to otherwise pander to presumed Democrat constituencies. (Unless, of course, that His- panic is named Ted Cruz, in which case they would pre- fer anybody else except Donald Trump.)

But Republican pandering, aside from being shame- ful, never works; if the election comes down to who can promise the most federal largesse to favored groups, Republicans can never outbid the Democrats—and they shouldn't try in any event. Bluntly put, identity politics is dressed-up racism. It has no place in the Republican Party—period.

But there is in our recent political history an electoral success that shows why Trump is a candidate who can restore Republican fortunes.

Think of Arnold Schwarzenegger. California used to be called "Reagan country." From 1952 through 1988, California was a reliable Republican state in presidential elections, going Democrat only once, in 1964. By the time Schwarzenegger ran for governor in 2003, California Republicans had almost become an endangered species. Yet Schwarzenegger won his election and was reelected governor as a Republican. Why? It wasn't his policies—in fact, many of his policies were thwarted by the Democrat legislature and those that weren't were, in their California context, unremarkable. In truth, once elected, Arnold as the "Governator" moved leftward to the moderate side of the party, eventually meeting with the inevitable political unpopularity that is a trademark of Republican moderates. Yet in the beginning he was elected because he had a persona that brought him voters from far outside what had become a shrinking Republican field. Trump has that same appeal. And Trump has advantages that Schwarzenegger did not have. If elected president, Trump would have a Republican Congress. Schwarzenegger's wife, when he was a governor, was Maria Shriver, a Kennedy and a liberal Democrat who played a major role in the administration. Trump would have no such divisions of political power. Schwarzenegger's first electoral victory was marked by a surge in California Republican Party registrations. A similar surge could happen on a national scale with Donald Trump—but Trump could also follow that up with policy successes that could make those new Republican voters stick, and even increase their number. Certainly that's *not* something that the current Republican congressional leadership is likely to do.

Voters elected Republican majorities in the United States House and Senate in 2014 with the expectation of change. But the only change they've seen is that Republicans who used to complain that action was impossible because they didn't have the votes, now say that they shouldn't take action at all. The Republican Congress has been a do-nothing, go-along-with-Obama Congress.

If that is what the Republican Party is going to be, why should anyone vote for the party's candidates? Why not just vote for Democrats who at least aren't ashamed of governing according to their own liberal principles?

The fact is, for the most part, the United States really only has one political party today—it's the Establishment Party and it's made up of the Democrats and a great many Republicans. That's bad for the country. We need two strong political parties that honestly and openly represent opposing views and contest for the support of the American people. In the words of Ronald Reagan, the GOP should be the party not of what Reagan disdained as "fraternal order" Republicans and "pale pastels" (or so-called "compassionate conservatism") but rather a party of "bold colors."

I believe that Donald Trump, as president, will not only make America great again, he will remake the Republican Party as a true conservative party open to everyone who believes, like Reagan did, that America can be, and should be, a shining city on a hill, a land of hope and opportunity, of economic prosperity, of safety and security. A nation where everyone is treated as what they really are—Americans one and all—not divided, as the Left loves to do—by race, ethnicity, and, these days, even sex and sexual preferences. We need another Reagan Revolution within the Republican Party. Trump can deliver it.

America Needs a Champion

You know, when President Obama was elected, I said, "Well, the one thing, I think he'll do well. I think he'll be a great cheerleader for the country. I think he'd be a great spirit." He was vibrant. He was young. I really thought that he would be a great cheerleader.

He's not a leader. That's true. You're right about that. But he wasn't a cheerleader. He's actually a negative force. He's been a negative force. He wasn't a cheerleader; he was the opposite.

We need somebody that can take the brand of the United States and make it great again. It's not great again. We need—we need somebody—we need somebody that literally will take this country and make it great again. We can do that.

—Donald Trump, announcing his presidential campaign, June 16, 2015

★ ★ ★

Running for president, Ronald Reagan said, "More than anything else, I want my candidacy to unify our country; to renew the American spirit and sense of purpose. I want to carry our message to every American, regardless of party affiliation, who is a member of this community of shared values."

Trump wants to unify America as well, rallying our fellow citizens to the restoration of American greatness.

"America doesn't win anymore," says Trump. He believes, passionately, that we "need somebody that can take the brand of the United States and make it great again." Trump is an old-style patriot, educated in part at a military school, whose family has lived the American dream in a gargantuan way; and as he has lived the American dream, he believes in traditional American values. He is not ashamed of America, as Obama often seems to be. He doesn't think that America needs to be fundamentally transformed into something else, as Obama apparently does.

Unlike Hillary Clinton, Trump has made his living in the private sector. Unlike her, he did not grow wealthy through having a presidential spouse and from being one of the bigshots of the Washington Cartel. Unlike her and Obama, his political roots do not lie with the perpetually aggrieved radical Left.

Like Ronald Reagan—who became a Republican only four years before his election as the Republican governor of California—Trump has been a Democrat and supported Democrats. It is curious that Establishment Republicans always insist they want to appeal for the votes of Democrats but condemned Reagan and Trump for their past support of Democrats. Reagan biographer Steven F. Hayward noted this in his account of the 1976 Ford-Reagan battle for the GOP presidential nomination: "During the Texas campaign Reagan began using a signature line in his appeal for crossover votes: 'I was a Democrat most of my adult life.' Ford and the Establishment professed outrage. Imagine! Seeking Democratic votes!"

Trump's Establishment Republican critics today, seemingly having learned nothing from Reagan, are making exactly the same argument that was being made against Reagan—expressing outrage at Trump's Democrat past. Safe to say, as with Reagan, conservatives in the base simply don't care.

But whether he has been a Republican or a Democrat, most of all Donald Trump has supported America, spending decades and an entire career literally building our nation's prosperity. Now he wants to take on the biggest building project one can imagine: making America great again. That starts with leadership. It starts with being a champion of the country you love.

I asked Donald Trump what his conception of being a leader was, and he replied:

> A leader is somebody that people follow and the reason they follow is respect. Or, unfortunately, the word fear can also be used. But the true leaders are people that can lead because of the fact that they are respected. And the primary way I found, I've seen over the years, the people that are most respected—and the easiest way to get respect—is to win. When you win people automatically gravitate to you. And it's a little bit like a football coach. You know, you can get a really tough football coach, and he can be a real rough guy. But if he starts losing all of the games he's not going to get away with

it. So respect is something that is very interesting but leadership is something that is a very interesting word and actually a very complex word in many respects. But I have just noticed over the years that the primary way that you get that leadership is through winning.

So when Donald Trump says he wants to make American win again—win in trade negotiations, win against our enemies, win as an economy—he's saying exactly what he means. And if you think that all American presidents, and candidates, want their country to win, you'd be wrong. Take for example Barack Obama. As Dinesh D'Souza argued in his book *America: Imagine a World without Her*,

> Obama is the architect of American decline, and progressivism is the ideology of American suicide. Here's a way to think about what Obama and the progressives are doing. Imagine if they were in charge of a basketball team with a fifty-year track record of success. We had them as coaches to keep the team winning. Yet they designed plays to ensure the

team would lose. They didn't do so because they hated the team, but because they thought it was wrong for the team to win so much. The long previous record of victories, they argued, was based on exploitation, and it would be better for everyone if our team wasn't so dominant. If we had such a coaching staff, there is little doubt that we would get rid of them. We would ask ourselves why we hired them in the first place.

Even though we currently have such a coach, decline is not an inevitability; decline is a choice. We don't have to let Obama and the progressives take us down. We certainly don't have to hire another coach who is like Obama. Do we want to live in a country that no longer matters, where the American dream is a paltry and shrunken thing, where bitter complaint substitutes for real influence in the world, where we can no longer expect our children to live better than we do?

Dinesh D'Souza's warning has been well heeded by Donald Trump. He wants to be the coach who takes America to victories. He wants to end what has become the standard Democrat position of apologizing for America, the idea of "blaming America first" which was popular in the Carter era, but has accelerated mightily in the Obama years. Obama, in fact, has made apologizing for America a focal point of his presidency.

For example, here are five examples of the Obama insistence on apologizing for America from a single two-month span first recorded by talk radio and Fox News host Sean Hannity and highlighted by the Washington Free Beacon:

- April 3, 2009, in Strasbourg, France: "In America, there's a failure to appreciate Europe's leading role in the world. Instead of celebrating your dynamic union and seeking to partner with you to meet common challenges, there have been times where America has shown arrogance and been dismissive, even derisive."
- April 6, 2009, in Ankara, Turkey: "Another issue that confronts all democracies as they move to the future is how we deal with the past. The United States is still working

through some of our own darker periods in our history."

- April 17, 2009, in Port of Spain, Trinidad and Tobago: "While the United States has done much to promote peace and prosperity in the hemisphere, we have at times been disengaged, and at times we sought to dictate our terms."

- April 20, 2009, at CIA Headquarters in Langley, Virginia: "Don't be discouraged that we have to acknowledge potentially we've made some mistakes. That's how we learn."

- May 21, 2009, at the National Archives in Washington, D.C.: "Unfortunately, faced with an uncertain threat, our government made a series of hasty decisions.... I also believe that all too often our government made decisions based on fear rather than foresight; that all too often our government trimmed facts and evidence to fit ideological predispositions. Instead of strategically applying our power and our principles, too often we set those principles aside as luxuries that we could no longer afford. And during this season of fear, too many of us—Democrats and Republicans, politicians, journalists, and citizens—fell silent. In other words, we went off course."

Catch those descriptions of America by its current president? Its "coach"? America is "dismissive," "has shown arrogance," is "still working through some of our own darker periods in our history," and has "been disengaged, and at times we sought to dictate our terms." America has "made some mistakes" and "made a series of hasty decisions... based on fear rather than foresight" so "we went off course."

These are the words of, as Dinesh D'Souza would say, a coach who does not want America to win; of a coach who thinks that other countries should take the lead even if they aren't capable of doing so; a coach who believes that an America that doesn't win is somehow in both America's—and the world's—best interests. These are hardly the words of inspiring American presidents from both political parties—presidents with names like Lincoln, Roosevelt, Kennedy, or Reagan.

In September 2015, a full 62 percent of Americans polled by NBC and the *Wall Street Journal* said the country was headed in the wrong direction. With leadership like Obama's, who could blame them? And does anyone honestly think that Hillary would be better, that she would chart a substantially different course from her predecessor in whose administration she served? Both Obama and Hillary come from the radical Left. Both have a predisposition to believe that America is the world's problem, not a force for good. Both are cynical enough to do everything they can to divide Americans for electoral gain, and to advance what they see as the progressive cause: whether it is campaigning against a mythical Republican war on women or raising racial tensions to a pitch not seen since the riots of the 1960s.

Donald Trump's view of America is entirely different. He does not come from the radical Left. He might be a billionaire, but he speaks for the common American:

> I love America. And when you love something, you protect it passionately—fiercely, even. We are the greatest country the world has ever known. I make no apologies for this country,

my pride in it, or my desire to see us become strong and rich again. After all, wealth funds our freedom. But for too long we've been pushed around, used by other countries, and ill-served by politicians in Washington who measure their success by how rapidly they can expand the federal debt, and your tax burden, with their favorite government programs.

American can do better. I think we deserve the best.

America *can* do better. America *does* deserve the best. Trump believes, as most Americans traditionally have, that we are a country set apart, an exceptional country, a country founded on principles of freedom and liberty.

It is a country that we need to make great again—not just for ourselves but for generations to come.

Donald Trump is committed to that vision—and he is better equipped than anyone else to carry it out.

In 2016, and in years to come, America will need a champion. Donald Trump is that champion.

Acknowledgments

This project would not have happened without the kind assistance of the man of many talents who is David Limbaugh. A serious man of great good humor, he took the time away from his own projects, for which I am more than appreciative.

My thanks as well to Harry Crocker, my editor at Regnery, managing editor Maria Ruhl, and all of their wonderful colleagues known and unknown who supplied the idea for this project.

Without the *American Spectator*, its indomitable founder and editor in chief R. Emmett Tyrrell Jr., and editorial director Wlady Pleszczynski, I would not have had the opportunity to meet Donald Trump and get to know the person as opposed to the media stereotype. For that a particular thanks.

To my extended family (in order or I will be in trouble)—cousins Judy Teuber, Suzanne Teuber Arnau, Jane Teuber, Beth Teuber, and Bruce Teuber, along with Joe Arnau, Bruce McAlpine, and the younger generation of Michele, Doc, Cheryl, Greg, Colin, Maeve, Adrienne, and Peter—thanks for taking charge of Mom so that I could use some Thanksgiving time to write in the quiet. And no, they are not all Trump supporters—or even conservatives!—but I'm working on them.

And last but not least, thanks to Donald Trump. He has stepped into a fray he does not need, is subjected to relentless attacks that are as base as they are untrue, and stays true to his love for an America that allows all of us to live our individual lives in freedom and liberty as we see fit.

What Trump Really Believes

Five Official Position Papers from the Campaign

★ Immigration

★ U.S.-China Trade

★ Veterans

★ Second Amendment Rights

★ Tax Reform

Immigration Reform That Will Make America Great Again

The Three Core Principles of Donald J. Trump's Immigration Plan

When politicians talk about "immigration reform" they mean: amnesty, cheap labor and open borders. The Schumer-Rubio immigration bill was nothing more than a giveaway to the corporate patrons who run both parties.

Real immigration reform puts the needs of working people first — not wealthy globetrotting donors. We are the only country in the world whose immigration system puts the needs of other nations ahead of our own. That must change. Here are the three core principles of real immigration reform:

1. A nation without borders is not a nation. There must be a wall across the southern border.

2. A nation without laws is not a nation. Laws passed in accordance with our Constitutional system of government must be enforced.

3. A nation that does not serve its own citizens is not a nation. Any immigration plan must improve jobs, wages and security for all Americans.

Make Mexico Pay For The Wall

For many years, Mexico's leaders have been taking advantage of the United States by using illegal immigration to export the crime and poverty in their own country (as well as in other Latin American countries). They have even published pamphlets on how to illegally immigrate to the United States. The costs for the United States have been extraordinary: U.S. taxpayers have been asked to pick up hundreds of billions in healthcare costs, housing costs, education costs, welfare costs, etc. Indeed, the annual cost of free tax credits alone paid to illegal immigrants quadrupled to $4.2 billion in 2011. The effects on jobseekers have also been disastrous, and black Americans have been particularly harmed.

The impact in terms of crime has been tragic. In recent weeks, the headlines have been covered with cases of criminals who crossed our border illegally only to go on to commit horrific crimes against Americans. Most recently, an illegal immigrant from Mexico, with a long arrest record, is charged with breaking into a 64 year-old woman's home, crushing her skull and eye sockets with a hammer, raping her, and murdering her. The Police Chief in Santa Maria says the "blood trail" leads straight to Washington.

In 2011, the Government Accountability Office found that there were a shocking 3 million arrests attached to the incarcerated alien population, including tens of thousands of violent beatings, rapes and murders.

Meanwhile, Mexico continues to make billions on not only our bad trade deals but also relies heavily on the billions of dollars in remittances sent from illegal immigrants in the United States back to Mexico ($22 billion in 2013 alone).

In short, the Mexican government has taken the United States to the cleaners. They are responsible for this problem, and they must help pay to clean it up.

The cost of building a permanent border wall pales mightily in comparison to what American taxpayers spend every single year on dealing with the fallout of illegal immigration on their communities, schools and unemployment offices.

Mexico must pay for the wall and, until they do, the United States will, among other things: impound all remittance payments derived from illegal wages; increase fees on all temporary visas issued to Mexican CEOs and diplomats (and if necessary cancel them); increase fees on all border crossing cards — of which

we issue about 1 million to Mexican nationals each year
(a major source of visa overstays); increase fees on all
NAFTA worker visas from Mexico (another major
source of overstays); and increase fees at ports of entry
to the United States from Mexico [Tariffs and foreign
aid cuts are also options]. We will not be taken advantage of anymore.

Defend the Laws and Constitution of the United States

America will only be great as long as America remains a
nation of laws that lives according to the Constitution.
No one is above the law. The following steps will return
to the American people the safety of their laws, which
politicians have stolen from them:

Triple the number of ICE officers. As the President of the
ICE Officers' Council explained in Congressional testi-
mony: "Only approximately 5,000 officers and agents
within ICE perform the lion's share of ICE's immigration
mission ... Compare that to the Los Angeles Police
Department at approximately 10,000 officers. Approximately 5,000 officers in ICE cover 50 states, Puerto Rico
and Guam, and are attempting to enforce immigration

law against 11 million illegal aliens already in the interior of the United States. Since 9-11, the U.S. Border Patrol has tripled in size, while ICE's immigration enforcement arm, Enforcement and Removal Operations (ERO), has remained at relatively the same size." This will be funded by accepting the recommendation of the Inspector General for Tax Administration and eliminating tax credit payments to illegal immigrants.

Nationwide e-verify. This simple measure will protect jobs for unemployed Americans.

Mandatory return of all criminal aliens. The Obama Administration has released 76,000 aliens from its custody with criminal convictions since 2013 alone. All criminal aliens must be returned to their home countries, a process which can be aided by canceling any visas to foreign countries which will not accept their own criminals, and making it a separate and additional crime to commit an offense while here illegally.

Detention—not catch-and-release. Illegal aliens apprehended crossing the border must be detained until they are sent home, no more catch-and-release.

Defund sanctuary cities. Cut-off federal grants to any city which refuses to cooperate with federal law enforcement.

Enhanced penalties for overstaying a visa. Millions of people come to the United States on temporary visas but refuse to leave, without consequence. This is a threat to national security. Individuals who refuse to leave at the time their visa expires should be subject to criminal penalties; this will also help give local jurisdictions the power to hold visa overstays until federal authorities arrive. Completion of a visa tracking system — required by law but blocked by lobbyists — will be necessary as well.

Cooperate with local gang task forces. ICE officers should accompany local police departments conducting raids of violent street gangs like MS-13 and the 18th street gang, which have terrorized the country. All illegal aliens in gangs should be apprehended and deported. Again, quoting Chris Crane: "ICE Officers and Agents are forced to apply the Deferred Action for Childhood Arrivals (DACA) Directive, not to children in schools, but to adult inmates in jails. If an illegal-alien inmate simply claims eligibility, ICE is forced to release the alien back into the community. This includes serious criminals who have committed felonies, who have assaulted officers, and who prey on children…ICE officers should be required to place detainers on every illegal alien they encounter in jails and prisons, since these aliens not only violated immigration laws, but then went on to engage in activities that led to their arrest by police; ICE officers should be required to issue Notices to Appear to all illegal aliens with criminal convictions, DUI convictions, or a gang affiliation; ICE should be working with any state or local drug or gang task force that asks for such assistance."

End birthright citizenship. This remains the biggest magnet for illegal immigration. By a 2:1 margin, voters say it's the wrong policy, including Harry Reid who said "no sane country" would give automatic citizenship to the children of illegal immigrants.

Put American Workers First

Decades of disastrous trade deals and immigration policies have destroyed our middle class. Today, nearly 40% of black teenagers are unemployed. Nearly 30% of Hispanic teenagers are unemployed. For black Americans without high school diplomas, the bottom has fallen out: more than 70% were employed in 1960, compared to

less than 40% in 2000. Across the economy, the percentage of adults in the labor force has collapsed to a level
not experienced in generations. As CBS news wrote in a
piece entitled "America's incredible shrinking middle
class": "If the middle-class is the economic backbone of
America, then the country is developing osteoporosis."

The influx of foreign workers holds down salaries,
keeps unemployment high, and makes it difficult for poor
and working class Americans — including immigrants
themselves and their children — to earn a middle class
wage. Nearly half of all immigrants and their US-born
children currently live in or near poverty, including more
than 60 percent of Hispanic immigrants. Every year, we
voluntarily admit another 2 million new immigrants,
guest workers, refugees, and dependents, growing our
existing all-time historic record population of 42 million
immigrants. We need to control the admission of new
low-earning workers in order to: help wages grow, get
teenagers back to work, aid minorities' rise into the middle class, help schools and communities falling behind,
and to ensure our immigrant members of the national
family become part of the American dream.

Additionally, we need to stop giving legal immigrant
visas to people bent on causing us harm. From the 9/11

hijackers, to the Boston Bombers, and many others, our immigration system is being used to attack us. The President of the immigration caseworkers union declared in a statement on ISIS: "We've become the visa clearing-house for the world."

Here are some additional specific policy proposals for long-term reform:

Increase prevailing wage for H-1Bs. We graduate two times more Americans with STEM degrees each year than find STEM jobs, yet as much as two-thirds of entry-level hiring for IT jobs is accomplished through the H-1B program. More than half of H-1B visas are issued for the program's lowest allowable wage level, and more than eighty percent for its bottom two. Raising the prevailing wage paid to H-1Bs will force companies to give these coveted entry-level jobs to the existing domestic pool of unemployed native and immigrant workers in the U.S., instead of flying in cheaper workers from overseas. This will improve the number of black, Hispanic and female workers in Silicon Valley who have been passed over in favor of the H-1B program. Mark Zuckerberg's personal Senator, Marco Rubio, has a bill to triple H-1Bs that would decimate women and minorities.

Requirement to hire American workers first. Too many visas, like the H-1B, have no such requirement. In the year 2015, with 92 million Americans outside the workforce and incomes collapsing, we need companies to hire from the domestic pool of unemployed. Petitions for workers should be mailed to the unemployment office, not USCIS.

End welfare abuse. Applicants for entry to the United States should be required to certify that they can pay for their own housing, healthcare and other needs before coming to the U.S.

Jobs program for inner city youth. The J-1 visa jobs program for foreign youth will be terminated and replaced with a resume bank for inner city youth provided to all corporate subscribers to the J-1 visa program.

Refugee program for American children. Increase standards for the admission of refugees and asylum-seekers to crack down on abuses. Use the monies saved on expensive refugee programs to help place American children without parents in safer homes and communities, and to improve community safety in high crime neighborhoods in the United States.

Immigration moderation. Before any new green cards are issued to foreign workers abroad, there will be a pause where employers will have to hire from the domestic pool of unemployed immigrant and native workers. This will help reverse women's plummeting workplace participation rate, grow wages, and allow record immigration levels to subside to more moderate historical averages.

Reforming the U.S.-China Trade Relationship to Make America Great Again

How We Got Here:
Washington Politicians Let China Off the Hook

In January 2000, President Bill Clinton boldly promised China's inclusion in the World Trade Organization (WTO) "is a good deal for America. Our products will gain better access to China's market, and every sector from agriculture, to telecommunications, to automobiles. But China gains no new market access to the United States." None of what President Clinton promised came true. Since China joined the WTO, Americans have witnessed the closure of more than 50,000 factories and the loss of tens of millions of jobs. It was <u>not</u> a good deal for America then and it's a bad deal now. It <u>is</u> a typical example of how politicians in Washington have failed our country.

<u>The most important component of our China policy is leadership and strength at the negotiating table.</u> We have been too afraid to protect and advance American interests and to challenge China to live up to its obligations. We need smart negotiators who will serve the interests of American workers — not Wall Street insiders that want to move U.S. manufacturing and investment offshore.

The Goal of the Trump Plan:
Fighting for American Businesses and Workers

America has always been a trading nation. Under the Trump administration trade will flourish. However, for free trade to bring prosperity to America, it must also be fair trade. Our goal is not protectionism but accountability. America fully opened its markets to China but China has not reciprocated. Its Great Wall of Protectionism uses unlawful tariff and non-tariff barriers to keep American companies out of China and to tilt the playing field in their favor.

If you give American workers a level playing field, they will win. At its heart, this plan is a negotiating strategy to bring fairness to our trade with China. The results will be huge for American businesses and workers. Jobs and factories will stop moving offshore and instead stay here at home. The economy will boom. The steps outlined in this plan will make that a reality.

When Donald J. Trump is president, China will be on notice that America is back in the global leadership business and that their days of currency manipulation and cheating are over. We will cut a better deal with China that helps American businesses and workers compete.

The Trump Plan Will Achieve the Following Goals:

1. Bring China to the bargaining table by immediately declaring it a currency manipulator.

2. Protect American ingenuity and investment by forcing China to uphold intellectual property laws and stop their unfair and unlawful practice of forcing U.S. companies to share proprietary technology with Chinese competitors as a condition of entry to China's market.

3. Reclaim millions of American jobs and reviving American manufacturing by putting <u>an end to China's illegal export subsidies and lax labor and environmental standards</u>. No more sweatshops or pollution havens stealing jobs from American workers.

4. Strengthen our negotiating position by <u>lowering our corporate tax rate</u> to keep American companies and jobs here at home, <u>attacking our debt and deficit</u> so China cannot use financial blackmail against us, and <u>bolstering the U.S. military presence</u> in the East and South China Seas to discourage Chinese adventurism.

Details of Donald J. Trump's US China Trade Plan:

Declare China A Currency Manipulator

We need a president who will not succumb to the financial blackmail of a Communist dictatorship. President Obama's Treasury Department has repeatedly refused to brand China a currency manipulator — a move that would force China to stop these unfair practices or face tough countervailing duties that level the playing field.

Economists estimate the Chinese yuan is undervalued by anywhere from 15% to 40%. This grossly undervalued yuan gives Chinese exporters a huge advantage while imposing the equivalent of a heavy tariff on U.S. exports to China. Such currency manipulation, in concert with China's other unfair practices, has resulted in chronic U.S. trade deficits, a severe weakening of the U.S. manufacturing base and the loss of tens of millions of American jobs.

In a system of truly free trade and floating exchange rates like a Trump administration would support, America's massive trade deficit with China would not persist. On day one of the Trump administration the U.S. Treasury Department will designate China as a currency manipulator. This will begin a process that imposes appropriate countervailing duties on artificially cheap

Chinese products, defends U.S. manufacturers and workers, and revitalizes job growth in America. We must stand up to China's blackmail and reject corporate America's manipulation of our politicians. The U.S. Treasury's designation of China as a currency manipulator will force China to the negotiating table and open the door to a fair — and far better — trading relationship.

End China's Intellectual Property Violations

China's ongoing theft of intellectual property may be the greatest transfer of wealth in history. This theft costs the U.S. over $300 billion and millions of jobs each year. China's government ignores this rampant cybercrime and, in other cases, actively encourages or even sponsors it –without any real consequences. China's cyber lawlessness threatens our prosperity, privacy and national security. <u>We will enforce stronger protections against Chinese hackers and counterfeit goods and our responses to Chinese theft will be swift, robust, and unequivocal.</u>

The Chinese government also forces American companies like Boeing, GE, and Intel to transfer proprietary technologies to Chinese competitors as a condition of entry into the Chinese market. Such de facto intellectual property theft represents a brazen violation of WTO and international rules. China's forced technology transfer policy is absolutely ridiculous. Going forward, <u>we will adopt a zero tolerance policy on intellectual property theft and forced technology transfer</u>. If China wants to trade with America, they must agree to stop stealing and to play by the rules.

Eliminate China's Illegal Export Subsidies And Other Unfair Advantages

Chinese manufacturers and other exporters receive numerous illegal export subsidies from the Chinese government. These include–in direct contradiction to WTO rules–free or nearly free rent, utilities, raw materials, and many other services. China's state-run banks routinely extend loans these enterprises at below market rates or without the expectation they will be repaid. China even offers them illegal tax breaks or rebates as well as cash bonuses to stimulate exports.

China's illegal export subsidies intentionally distorts international trade and damages other countries' exports by giving Chinese companies an unfair advantage. From textile and steel mills in the Carolinas to the Gulf Coast's shrimp and fish industries to the Midwest manufacturing belt and California's agribusiness, China's disregard for WTO rules hurt every corner of America.

The U.S. Trade Representative recently filed yet another complaint with the WTO accusing China of cheating on our trade agreements by subsidizing its exports. The Trump administration will not wait for an international body to tell us what we already know. To gain negotiating leverage, we will pursue the WTO case and aggressively highlight and expose these subsidies.

China's woeful lack of reasonable environmental and labor standards represent yet another form of unacceptable export subsidy. How can American manufacturers, who must meet very high standards, possibly compete with Chinese companies that care nothing about their workers or the environment? We will challenge China to join the 21st Century when it comes to such standards.

The Trump Plan Will Strengthen Our Negotiating Position

As the world's most important economy and consumer of goods, America must always negotiate trade agreements from strength. Branding China as a currency manipulator and exposing their unfair trade practices is not enough. In order to further strengthen our negotiating leverage, the Trump plan will:

1. Lower the corporate tax rate to 15% to unleash American ingenuity here at home and make us more globally competitive. This tax cut puts our rate 10 percentage points below China and 20 points below our current burdensome rate that pushes companies and jobs offshore.

2. Attack our debt and deficit by vigorously eliminating waste, fraud and abuse in the Federal government, ending redundant government programs, and growing the economy to increase tax revenues. Closing the deficit and reducing our debt will mean China cannot blackmail us with our own Treasury bonds.

3. Strengthen the U.S. military and deploying it appropriately in the East and South China Seas. These actions will discourage Chinese adventurism that imperils American interests in Asia and shows our strength as we begin renegotiating our trading relationship with China. A strong military presence will be a clear signal to China and other nations in Asia and around the world that America is back in the global leadership business.

Veterans Administration Reforms That Will Make America Great Again

The Goals of Donald J. Trump's Veterans Plan

The current state of the Department of Veterans Affairs (VA) is absolutely unacceptable. Over 300,000 veterans died waiting for care. Corruption and incompetence were excused. Politicians in Washington have done too little too slowly to fix it. This situation can never happen again, and when Donald J. Trump is president, it will be fixed — fast.

The guiding principle of the Trump plan is ensuring veterans have convenient access to the best quality care. To further this principle, the Trump plan will decrease wait times, improve healthcare outcomes, and facilitate a seamless transition from service into civilian life.

The Trump Plan Will:

1. Ensure our veterans get the care they need wherever and whenever they need it. No more long drives. No more waiting for backlogs. No more excessive red tape. Just the care and support they earned with their service to our country.

2. Support the whole veteran, not just their physical health care, but also by addressing their invisible wounds, investing in our service members' post-active duty success, transforming the VA to meet the needs of 21st century

service members, and better meeting the needs of our
female veterans.

3. Make the VA great again by firing the corrupt and incompetent VA executives who let our veterans down, by
modernizing the VA, and by empowering the doctors and
nurses to ensure our veterans receive the best care available in a timely manner.

The Trump Plan Gives Veterans the Freedom to Choose and Forces the VA to Compete for Their Dollars

Politicians in Washington have tried to fix the VA by
holding hearings and blindly throwing money at the
problem. None of it has worked. In fact, wait times were
50% higher this summer than they were a year ago.
That's because the VA lacks the right leadership and
management. It's time we stop trusting Washington politicians to fix the problems and empower our veterans to
vote with their feet.

Under a Trump Administration, all veterans eligible
for VA health care can bring their veteran's ID card to
any doctor or care facility that accepts Medicare to get
the care they need immediately. Our veterans have earned

the freedom to choose better or more convenient care from the doctor and facility of their choice. The power to choose will stop the wait time backlogs and force the VA to improve and compete if the department wants to keep receiving veterans' healthcare dollars. The VA will become more responsive to veterans, develop more efficient systems, and improve the quality of care because it will have no other choice.

The Trump Plan Treats the Whole Veteran

We must care for the whole veteran, not just their physical health. We must recognize that today's veterans have very different needs than those of the Greatest Generation.

The Trump Plan Will:

1. Increase funding for post-traumatic stress disorder (PTSD), traumatic brain injury and suicide prevention services to address our veterans' invisible wounds. Service members are five times more likely to develop depression than civilians. They are almost fifteen times more likely to develop PTSD than civilians. This funding will help provide more and better counseling and care. More funding will also support research on best practices and state of the art treatments to keep our veterans alive, healthy and whole. With these steps, the Trump plan will help the veteran community put the unnecessary stigma surrounding mental health behind them and instead encourage acceptance and treatment in our greater society.

2. Increase funding for job training and placement services (including incentives for companies hiring veterans), educational support and business loans. All Americans agree that we must do everything we can to help put our service men and women on a path to success as they leave active duty by collaborating with the many successful non-profit organizations that are already helping. Service members have learned valuable skills in the military but many need help understanding how to apply those skills in civilian life. Others know how to apply those skills but need help connecting with good jobs to support their families. Still others have an entrepreneurial spirit and are ready to start creating jobs and growing the economy. The Trump plan will strengthen existing programs or replace them with more effective ones to address these needs and to get our veterans working.

3. Transform the VA to meet the needs of 21st century service members. Today's veterans have very different needs than those of the generations that came before them. The VA must adapt to meet the needs of this generation of younger, more diverse veterans. The Trump plan will expand VA services for female veterans and ensure the VA is providing the right support for this new generation of veterans.

4. Better support our women veterans. The fact that many VA hospitals don't permanently staff OBGYN doctors shows an utter lack of respect for the growing number female veterans. Under the Trump plan, every VA hospital in the country will be fully equipped with OBGYN and other women's health services. In addition, women veterans can always choose a different OBGYN in their community using their veteran's ID card.

The Trump Plan Will Make the VA Great Again

The VA health care program is a disaster. Some candidates want to get rid of it, but our veterans need the VA to be there for them and their families. That's why the Trump plan will:

1. Fire the corrupt and incompetent VA executives that let our veterans down. Under a Trump Administration, there will be no job security for VA executives that enabled or overlooked corruption and incompetence. They're fired. New leadership will focus the VA staff on delivering timely, top quality care and other services to our nation's veterans. Under a Trump Administration, exposing and addressing the VA's inefficiencies and shortcomings will be rewarded, not punished.

2. End waste, fraud and abuse at the VA. The Trump plan will ensure the VA is spending its dollars wisely to provide the greatest impact for veterans and hold administrators accountable for irresponsible spending and abuse. The days of $6.3 million for statues and fountains at VA facilities and $300,000 for a manager to move 140 miles are over. The Trump plan will clean up the VA's finances so the current VA budget provides more and better care than it does now.

3. Modernize the VA. A VA with 20th century technology cannot serve 21st century service members and their needs. The VA has been promising to modernize for years without real results. The Trump plan will make it happen by accelerating and expanding investments in state of the art technology to deliver best-in-class care quickly and effectively. All veterans should be able to conveniently schedule appointments, communicate with their doctors, and view accurate wait times with the push of a button.

4. Empower the caregivers to ensure our veterans receive quality care quickly. Caregivers should be able to easily streamline treatment plans across departments and utilize telehealth tools to better serve their patients. As we have seen from the private sector, the potential for new, innovative technology is endless. Abandoning the wasteful and archaic mindset of the public sector will give way to tremendously effective veteran healthcare.

5. Hire more veterans to care for veterans. The more veterans we have working at the VA, the better the VA will be. They understand the unique challenges facing their community. To increase the number of veterans hired by the VA, this plan will add an additional 5 points to the qualifying scores of veterans applying for VA jobs.

6. Embed satellite VA clinics in rural and other underserved areas. The Trump Administration will embed satellite VA clinics within hospitals and other care facilities in rural and other underserved areas. This step will ensure veterans have easy access to care and local hospitals and care facilities can handle the influx of patients without backlogs while tapping the specialized knowledge of VA health specialists.

Protecting Our Second Amendment Rights Will Make America Great Again

Donald J. Trump on the Right to Keep and Bear Arms

The Second Amendment to our Constitution is clear. The right of the people to keep and bear Arms shall not be infringed upon. Period.

The Second Amendment guarantees a fundamental right that belongs to all law-abiding Americans. The Constitution doesn't create that right — it ensures that the government can't take it away. Our Founding Fathers knew, and our Supreme Court has upheld, that the Second Amendment's purpose is to guarantee our right to defend ourselves and our families. This is about self-defense, plain and simple.

It's been said that the Second Amendment is America's first freedom. That's because the Right to Keep and Bear Arms protects all our other rights. We are the only country in the world that has a Second Amendment. Protecting that freedom is imperative. Here's how we will do that:

Enforce The Laws On The Books

We need to get serious about prosecuting violent criminals. The Obama administration's record on that is abysmal. Violent crime in cities like Baltimore, Chicago and many others is out of control. Drug dealers and gang members are given a slap on the wrist and turned loose on the street. This needs to stop.

Several years ago there was a tremendous program in Richmond, Virginia called Project Exile. It said that if a violent felon uses a gun to commit a crime, you will be prosecuted in federal court and go to prison for five years — no parole or early release. Obama's former Attorney General, Eric Holder, called that a "cookie cutter" program. That's ridiculous. I call that program a success. Murders committed with guns in Richmond decreased by over 60% when Project Exile was in place — in the first two years of the program alone, 350 armed felons were taken off the street.

Why does that matter to law-abiding gun owners? Because they're the ones who anti-gun politicians and the media blame when criminals misuse guns. We need to bring back and expand programs like Project Exile and get gang members and drug dealers off the street. When we do, crime will go down and our cities and communities will be safer places to live.

Here's another important way to fight crime — empower law-abiding gun owners to defend themselves.

Law enforcement is great, they do a tremendous job, but they can't be everywhere all of the time. Our personal protection is ultimately up to us. That's why I'm a gun owner, that's why I have a concealed carry permit, and that's why tens of millions of Americans have concealed carry permits as well. It's just common sense. To make America great again, we're going to go after criminals and put the law back on the side of the lawabiding.

Fix Our Broken Mental Health System

Let's be clear about this. Our mental health system is broken. It needs to be fixed. Too many politicians have ignored this problem for too long.

All of the tragic mass murders that occurred in the past several years have something in common — there were red flags that were ignored. We can't allow that to continue. We need to expand treatment programs, because most people with mental health problems aren't violent, they just need help. But for those who are violent, a danger to themselves or others, we need to get them off the street before they can terrorize our communities. This is just common sense.

And why does this matter to law-abiding gun owners? Once again, because they get blamed by anti-gun politicians, gun control groups and the media for the acts of deranged madmen. When one of these tragedies occurs, we can count on two things: one, that opponents of gun rights will immediately exploit it to push their political agenda; and two, that none of their so-called "solutions" would have prevented the tragedy in the first place. They've even admitted it.

We need real solutions to address real problems. Not grandstanding or political agendas.

Defend The Rights of Law-Abiding Gun Owners

Gun and Magazine Bans. Gun and magazine bans are a total failure. That's been proven every time it's been tried. Opponents of gun rights try to come up with scary sounding phrases like "assault weapons", "military-style weapons" and "high capacity magazines" to confuse people. What they're really talking about are popular semi-automatic rifles and standard magazines that are owned by tens of millions of Americans. Law-abiding people should be allowed to own the firearm of their choice. The government has no business dictating what types of firearms good, honest people are allowed to own.

Background Checks. There has been a national background check system in place since 1998. Every time a person buys a gun from a federally licensed gun dealer — which is the overwhelming majority of all gun purchases — they go through a federal background check. Study after study has shown that very few criminals are stupid enough to try and pass a background check — they get their guns from friends/family members or by stealing them. So the overwhelming majority of people who go through background checks are law-abiding gun owners. When the system was created, gun owners were promised that it would be instant, accurate and fair. Unfortunately, that isn't the case today. Too many states are failing to put criminal and mental health records into the system — and it should go without saying that a system's only going to be as effective as the records that are put into it. What we need to do is fix the system we have and make it work as intended. What we don't need to do is expand a broken system.

National Right to Carry. The right of self-defense doesn't stop at the end of your driveway. That's why I have a concealed carry permit and why tens of millions of Americans do too. That permit should be valid in all

50 states. A driver's license works in every state, so it's common sense that a concealed carry permit should work in every state. If we can do that for driving — which is a privilege, not a right — then surely we can do that for concealed carry, which is a right, not a privilege.

Military Bases and Recruiting Centers. Banning our military from carrying firearms on bases and at recruiting centers is ridiculous. We train our military how to safely and responsibly use firearms, but our current policies leave them defenseless. To make America great again, we need a strong military. To have a strong military, we need to allow them to defend themselves.

Tax Reform That Will Make America Great Again

The Goals Of Donald J. Trump's Tax Plan

Too few Americans are working, too many jobs have been shipped overseas, and too many middle class families cannot make ends meet. This tax plan directly meets these challenges with four simple goals:

1. Tax relief for middle class Americans: In order to achieve the American dream, let people keep more money in their pockets and increase after-tax wages.

2. Simplify the tax code to reduce the headaches Americans face in preparing their taxes and let everyone keep more of their money.

3. Grow the American economy by discouraging corporate inversions, adding a huge number of new jobs, and making America globally competitive again.

4. Doesn't add to our debt and deficit, which are already too large.

The Trump Tax Plan Achieves These Goals

1. If you are single and earn less than $25,000, or married and jointly earn less than $50,000, you will not owe any income tax. That removes nearly 75 million households — over 50% — from the income tax rolls. They get a new one page form to send the IRS saying, "I win," those who would otherwise owe income taxes will save an average of nearly $1,000 each.

2. All other Americans will get a simpler tax code with four brackets — 0%, 10%, 20% and 25% — instead of the current seven. This new tax code eliminates the marriage penalty and the Alternative Minimum Tax (AMT) while providing the lowest tax rate since before World War II.

3. No business of any size, from a Fortune 500 to a mom and pop shop to a freelancer living job to job, will pay more than 15% of their business income in taxes. This lower rate makes corporate inversions unnecessary by making America's tax rate one of the best in the world.

4. No family will have to pay the death tax. You earned and saved that money for your family, not the government. You paid taxes on it when you earned it.

The Trump Tax Plan Is Revenue Neutral

The Trump tax cuts are fully paid for by:

1. Reducing or eliminating most deductions and loopholes available to the very rich.

2. A one-time deemed repatriation of corporate cash held overseas at a significantly discounted 10% tax rate, followed by an end to the deferral of taxes on corporate income earned abroad.

3. Reducing or eliminating corporate loopholes that cater to special interests, as well as deductions made unnecessary or redundant by the new lower tax rate on corporations and business income. We will also phase in a reasonable cap on the deductibility of business interest expenses.

Details of Donald J. Trump's Tax Plan

America needs a bold, simple and achievable plan based on conservative economic principles. This plan does that with needed tax relief for all Americans, especially the working poor and middle class, pro-growth tax reform for all sizes of businesses, and fiscally responsible steps to ensure this plan does not add to our enormous debt and deficit.

This plan simplifies the tax code by taking nearly 50% of current filers off the income tax rolls entirely and reducing the number of tax brackets from seven to four for everyone else. This plan also reduces or eliminates loopholes used by the very rich and special interests made unnecessary or redundant by the new lower tax rates on individuals and companies.

The Trump Tax Plan: A Simpler Tax Code for All Americans

When the income tax was first introduced, just <u>one</u> percent of Americans had to pay it. It was never intended as a tax most Americans would pay. The Trump plan eliminates the income tax for over 73 million households. 42 million households that currently file complex forms to determine they don't owe any income taxes will now file a one page form saving them time, stress, uncertainty and an average of $110 in preparation costs. Over 31 million households get the same simplification and keep on average nearly $1,000 of their hard-earned money.

For those Americans who will still pay the income tax, the tax rates will go from the current seven brackets to four simpler, fairer brackets that eliminate the marriage penalty and the AMT while providing the lowest tax rate since before World War II:

Income Tax Rate	Long Term Cap Gains/ Dividends Rate	Single Filers	Married Filers	Heads of Household
0%	0%	$0 to $25,000	$0 to $50,000	$0 to $37,500
10%	0%	$25,001 to $50,000	$50,001 to $100,000	$37,501 to $75,000
20%	15%	$50,001 to $150,000	$100,001 to $300,000	$75,001 to $225,000
25%	20%	$150,001 and up	$300,001 and up	$225,001 and up

With this huge reduction in rates, many of the current exemptions and deductions will become unnecessary or redundant. Those within the 10% bracket will keep all or most of their current deductions. Those within the 20% bracket will keep more than half of their current deductions. Those within the 25% bracket will keep fewer deductions. Charitable giving and mortgage interest deductions will remain unchanged for all taxpayers.

Simplifying the tax code and cutting every American's taxes will boost consumer spending, encourage savings and investment, and maximize economic growth.

Business Tax Reform to Encourage Jobs and Spur Economic Growth

Too many companies — from great American brands to innovative startups — are leaving America, either directly or through corporate inversions. The Democrats want to outlaw inversions, but that will never work. Companies leaving is not the disease, it is the symptom. Politicians in Washington have let America fall from the best corporate tax rate in the industrialized world in the 1980's (thanks to Ronald Reagan) to the worst rate in the industrialized world. That is unacceptable. Under the Trump plan, America will compete with the world and win by cutting the corporate tax rate to 15%, taking our rate from one of the worst to one of the best.

This lower tax rate cannot be for big business alone; it needs to help the small businesses that are the true engine of our economy. Right now, freelancers, sole proprietors, unincorporated small businesses and pass-through entities are taxed at the high personal income tax rates. This treatment stifles small businesses. It also stifles tax reform because efforts to reduce loopholes and deductions available to the very rich and special interests end up hitting small businesses and job creators as well. The Trump plan addresses this challenge head on with a new business income tax rate within the personal income tax code that matches the 15% corporate tax rate to help these businesses, entrepreneurs and freelancers grow and prosper.

These lower rates will provide a tremendous stimulus for the economy — significant GDP growth, a huge number of new jobs and an increase in after-tax wages for workers.

The Trump Tax Plan Ends the Unfair Death Tax

The death tax punishes families for achieving the American dream. Therefore, the Trump plan eliminates the death tax.

The Trump Tax Plan is Fiscally Responsible

The Trump tax cuts are fully paid for by:

1. Reducing or eliminating deductions and loopholes available to the very rich, starting by steepening the curve of the Personal Exemption Phaseout and the Pease Limitation on itemized deductions. The Trump plan also

phases out the tax exemption on life insurance interest for high-income earners, ends the current tax treatment of carried interest for speculative partnerships that do not grow businesses or create jobs and are not risking their own capital, and reduces or eliminates other loopholes for the very rich and special interests. These reductions and eliminations will not harm the economy or hurt the middle class. Because the Trump plan introduces a new business income rate within the personal income tax code, they will not harm small businesses either.

2. A one-time deemed repatriation of corporate cash held overseas at a significantly discounted 10% tax rate. Since we are making America's corporate tax rate globally competitive, it is only fair that corporations help make that move fiscally responsible. U.S.-owned corporations have as much as $2.5 trillion in cash sitting overseas. Some companies have been leaving cash overseas as a tax maneuver. Under this plan, they can bring their cash home and put it to work in America while benefitting from the newly-lowered corporate tax rate that is globally competitive and no longer requires parking cash overseas. Other companies have cash overseas for specific business units or activities. They can leave that cash overseas, but they will still have to pay the one-time repatriation fee.

3. An end to the deferral of taxes on corporate income earned abroad. Corporations will no longer be allowed to defer taxes on income earned abroad, but the foreign tax credit will remain in place because no company should face double taxation.

4. Reducing or eliminating some corporate loopholes that cater to special interests, as well as deductions made unnecessary or redundant by the new lower tax rate on corporations and business income. We will also phase in a reasonable cap on the deductibility of business interest expenses.